BEWARE OF THE WHORE

BEFORE HE/SHE DESTROYS ALL THAT GOD HAS BLESSED YOU WITH!

SCOTT LONGAS

www.scottlongas.com

Beware of the Whore

TABLE OF CONTENTS

Beware of the Whore

Beware of the Whore

Introduction

___WHORE___ ...

*A Deep Ditch; A Strange Man/
Woman is a Narrow pit of **EVIL***

*(Proverbs **23:27** whole chapter)*

This *IS* a <u>TRUE STORY</u>

Hello my friend, My name is Scott Longas. First
of all, I am not a *Celebrity,* or a *Childhood Actor*
writing a story about their life. Additionally, I am
not one of those *Renown Authors* writing another
one of those *Fairy Tales* with a *Happy Ending!*
You know the kind, the *Romantic Fiction Novels*
that make you want to go to the *Freezer,* and grab
a bowl of ice cream, with a sense of *Suspense and
Anticipation,* learn how the Handsome *Prince
Robert* saved the imprisoned *Princess Christine*
from the *Ruthless King.*

No, I am just your *average Person,* who (*like everyone else*) had some *Childhood Dreams, and wishes like you when I was a child, so you are thinking; why read this Story?* What is so special about my *Book*?

Well my friend, my *Book* is of the *Reality* type of *Story*! And to *cut to the chase*, I am the *Villain* in this story (*along with an *all too Familiar accomplice, That person I will get to in a minute*) The reason I chose to write this story is parallel to *alcoholic* writing a story of their life living as a alcohol abuser, and it's *Damaging effects* on their life and along with it, the damage it has caused in the relationship *with others as well*!

Except, in my case, my "Choice' of Poison was as toxic as is drugs, and alcohol! And, had the same damaging effects to myself and to anyone close in my life…So, I hope you read with an 'open mind", and get ready for some *important information* enclosed in my *Story*…But, do not go to the *Freezer* and get a *Bowl of Ice Cream* to take with you to read this Story…Instead, I suggest you grab your *Wedding Album* or a *Picture* of the person that you are presently in a *Promise of*

Marriage relationship with. *(Maybe even add a Glass of Wine to take with you)* And, get ready for a *Real Life* history lesson about *Love and Marriage.*

The information I will explain is my personal story may be more of significant importance to you than a *Fairy Tale!* Mainly because, if you had some of these same wishes that I had when you were a Child, hopefully *(with the information provided in this book)* I can Possibly keep you from *Losing them!*...

This story is about my *Personal Tragedy* which was caused by a *"Choice"* I made while living my *Dream.* The *"Choice'* that I made *Destroyed* my Childhood *Hopes and Dreams* worst than, well, *Death* itself!

I would like to share my story to all....for *Two Reasons*... *First,* in the attempt to hopefully answer the burning Question asked around town; *"What really happened to Scott Longas?"* *Secondly,* for the others, I will heed this book as "A WARNING" to all that had/have *Dreams of their own*...In this book; I will tell you the Story of how I achieved the *"American Dream".* You heard of it, hadn't you? The *Dream* to one day have that *Great Job or Career*, eventually meet and *marry* that '*Special Person*" to share the rest of your life with?

And, in the course of the marriage, be *blessed* with children, and, raise a family together? Well, that was *MY DREAM...*

But, I had no idea that through the course of living my *Dream*, I would slip into a *NIGHTMARE* that I could not wakeup from! Folks...

In this *Nightmare,* you will learn how I would make contact with one of the most "*Deadly Diseases*" that has been responsible for the Destruction of *Marriages* and *Relationships* all over this great country of ours.

The name of this "*Disease*" is called... *INFIDELITY!* Yes, yes, yes! And, the *Main Carrier* of this *type* of Disease is...*THE **WHORE**.* Yes folks, you will read in this story how **I** managed to destroy my **23** years of marriage by the "*Decision*" to choose a **WHORE***!* In addition, (*you will learn*) *the Devastating ripple effects* that came along with it. Now as I wrote in the introduction, this is a True story. And I mean the *Brutal TRUTH*! There will be no *Embellishing* remarks or statements in this book! I do not care for the *"Coward Authors"* whom write their *"True Memoirs"* and later reveal that their story only had a *"little bit'"* of the truth in the book's contents.

But, as you will read in this story, I will give you only *The Facts*! I will not be hiding anything in this book. Because, I *know that God* and my *Father* do not care for *Cowards*. I will be telling the *Whole Truth, Nothing but the Truth, so Help me God*!...

Now with that, I only changed some of the Names in this Book (to protect the Innocent, and *Not so Innocent*)

First, let's define the meaning of the word **"WHORE"**...Definition: ...*an offensive term for somebody who is regarded as <u>willing to set aside principles</u> or <u>personal integrity </u>in <u>order to obtain something, usually for selfish motives.</u>*

So now that we are clear on the *Specific* definition of the word **WHORE** I am referring to in my story.

Before we go any further into my story, I would like to ask YOU a Question?

*Did you ever want to hold a **Deadly Scorpion** in your hand? Knowing very well by attempting such an act, could result in a potentially lethal bite. But IF you ignored the Warning and "Chose" to make a conscious "Decision" to do it anyway, And while doing so, you ultimately received a Potentially Lethal bite. Should you be angry at the **Scorpion**? Or, are YOU to blame?*

Well, that is the theory of what My Story is all about. This is a story of a "*CHOICE*" that I made while in my **23** years of Marriage. Yes… I knew this could be *harmful* to my Marriage, But, I thought I would not get *BITTEN*! And as you will read, Not only did I get bit, but The VENOM that it contained infiltrated my life like a *match on Gasoline!*

You will also learn in this story how my 'Choice" destroyed everything in its path, similar to a *Killer Tornado* hitting a *Straw House.*

Yes, I opened the *Trap Door* to HELL, and jumped right in because of my *'Choice"*… As you read further in this story, I will not Blame *THE WHORE* for my downfall! Yes, although she played a role in the destruction of my marriage, ultimately… I *"chose her"*. And consequently, *I am the **only** person to blame!*

Now, not all Relationships are "A *Bed of Roses"*. But in my Relationship, I had it *All*… I was *blessed* with…*A Beautiful Wife, a Beautiful Daughter, a Wonderful Home in a Great Community, My own Business, Along with some Great Family and Friends*…I was involved in the local community. I even raised money for local charities. I was so respected by my Family, and Friends, and in our Community. I was even treated like a *Local Celebrity* around our town because *of the 'Honest, and Hard Work"* that I achieved! Yes, I was indeed blessed by GOD at the time. I received *everything* I ever wanted as a Child, and *More!*

Then, I made the *"CHOICE'* to be lured by *The WHORE*… And my life went into a *Downward Spiral* (*to this day*) I have not yet recovered from....I went from Rags to Riches to *RAGS* again, because of the "*CHOICE*" that I made. Let me go a little further to explain how *bad* things got for me...Before my fateful decision, My phone would ring *nonstop* from my family and friends just calling to say "*Hello*"... that same Phone today is now *silent!* The only calls I receive today are from the *Collection Department*!

Yes Folks, all of *my Family, Friends,* and most of all...*My little Girl* want nothing to do with me because of my '*CHOICE*"! Yes friend and *Infidelity* is the reason for my downfall!

This leads to the reason I call INFIDELITY a "Disease". *Infidelity* is now reaching at *epidemic proportions* in our daily lives! Furthermore, this *Disease* is spreading into most of our Marriages and Relationships today. I am sure right now you could name off a list of Relationships and Marriages that were ruined in your circle of *Family* or *Friends* because of *Infidelity.* Am I right....And for what?
Maybe you're not having enough *Sex* in your marriage? Well, as you will read in this story, I found that the "*Grass isn't always Greener*" on

the other side as they say.   You could be in for a
Big Surprise (as I did) when you finally realize
you made a *Bad Choice* for *Straying* out on your
Relationship. Yes, the **WHORE** is lurking in your
local Bars, *Nightclubs*, *Websites*, even at your
Workplace, just waiting for their opportunity to
"STRIKE" at anytime!

And when **you** allow them into your life, they
WILL ruin *"everything"* God has blessed you
with! That is, *"if you make the CHOICE"*

Let me explain even further to you how bad
things got for me, *in 2003* my brother **Gary**
suffered and eventually passed away from *Acute
Leukemia.* And we as a family, watched Gary go
through some of the most grueling *chemotherapy
treatments* you could ever imagine … But for me,
after choosing *The WHORE,* I would have gladly
exchanged my fate for the same kind of Grueling
suffering that my brother endured instead of what
I will call…My Ultimate **HELL**!

So before you read any further… Let me ask you
another question…why did you buy this Book?
Did you want to read it because you are *curious of
its contents*? Or, is it because you are thinking

about *Cheating?* Or are you already in a *Cheating affair?* Or maybe…you *KNOW* someone that is?

Just look at how this *"Disease"* of *INFIDELITY* has left its lasting *ugly* mark in *U.S. History…*

John F. Kennedy, one of the most *Famous U.S. Presidents* of our time, is BEST known for his alleged "INFIDELITY" with *Marilyn Monroe… **Bill Clinton*** was also a *Great President.* But, he is also best known for his *"I did not have sexual relations with that woman"* statement! And honestly, that is a shame!   But that could have been prevented.

It was all because of the *"CHOICE"* that they made. Their *"Choice"* was to take a Bite of the *Forbidden Fruit,* and their *Fate* and *legacy* as President will *forever be etched in the History books…*My friend, the list could go on and on….

So, think about this….
What *"CHOICES"* will you make in this life that you would like to leave as a lasting impression of you and your accomplishments on this planet?

What will be your *Legacy?* Again, in writing this book *(with the help of GOD)* I am sending out a '*WARNING*" to those that are in a *Healthy* Relationship.

And (in the hopes) that they *do not* "Choose" the same path as I did (*THE* **WHORE**)....

Here is my Story. And, a "*WARNING*" to ALL!

CHAPTER 1 *(My Childhood)*

I WAS BORN ON APRIL 17, 1960 IN DETROIT MICHIGAN. With my older brothers Mark, and Gary and a young sister named Kathy. My Parents were ***James*** and ***Betty Longas***. My family lived in the rough streets of downtown Detroit known as the *Cass Corridor*. My father worked on the Lakes as a Chef.   My mother also worked *(to help raise this rather Big Family)*. My mother was a hard working Woman… she worked as a waitress at a local 'Greasy Spoon" in an area just a block from our apartment in the Cass Corridor.

My mother would serve some of the most *Classless Patrons* you would ever want to meet. Because, the Cass Corridor had the most *Crime, Drug dealers, Pimps, and Prostitute's* in the city of Detroit. While working and walking in our part of the neighborhood, you had to be aware of your surroundings. And, hopefully you had *Common Sense*. If not, you could be found face down in an alley somewhere, or be on the side of a *Milk Carton*!

My father worked as a baker and cook on a Lake Ship (*what company I do not know*) what I do know, was that my Father was the reason that we were raised with *Street Smarts* and with Toughness! My Father was a *Tough Guy*...He was Known by his **WWII** Buddies as the *"Painless Dentist" (in short, he could hit you so hard and fast that you would not realize that your teeth were missing!)* My father also served in both **WWII** and the *Korean War!* And because of the "Battles" he had to endure while serving our country overseas, my father also unfortunately had some "Alcohol Battles" at home that would cause him to have a *Bad Temper* at times...
He was intimidating looking. And we kids never want to get him angry! Heaven forbid if we ever got out of line, because the Tool of   discipline that my father used on us was called a *Backhand Slap*. My father called it a *"Sly-Rap" (No, this was not a Rap Song...but a "Smack in the Face" With the back of his hand)* so, because of my father's tool of discipline, we knew to mind our **P's** and **Q's**. When it came to us even thinking about getting into trouble, we were not afraid of attracting the Police, we were afraid of our own

"Jimmy the Greek". Because of our father we were able to stay out of trouble in this tough area known as the Cass Corridor…Our mother and father met each other in New York City…She was (*at the time of their meeting*) in a physically abusive relationship with her current boyfriend. My mother and her Boyfriend also had a Son together (*they never married*) His name was *George*. My father took a liking to my mother. One Particular day, she informed my father that she was again threatened by her boyfriend. But this time, he was threatening her with a *Knife!*

My father that night took my mother and her Son George to stay with him. Then, my father paid her boyfriend *"A Visit"*… Well I will not go into the details of what happened that day when they met. I will only tell you that this *Woman Beater* never bothered her again! After that event, both of my parents left *New York* to start a life together in *Michigan*…My mother left her son George with her sister in Pittsburg PA (*my father wanted to bring George with them, but my mother thought he would be better off with her sister*) Because my mother was young, and wanted to start a *New Life* with my father in Michigan. When my parents arrived in Michigan, they settled in an apartment in the city of Detroit (*known as the Cass Corridor*). Later, they would start a family and had four children…Both of my parents had to get jobs and work long hours to support all of us.

Lack of money was always an issue in our household, and would cause some pressure in the home. Most of the arguments that my parents would have during their relationship would always involve the lack of *Money*…When I was a little boy of *Eight*, I was regularly attend *Bible Study* at a local Church to establish a connection with this person I heard a lot about, Named *GOD*. I was so intrigued to learn about God. Because I remember my mother would always say *"with the help of GOD"* to us whenever any of us kids would leave the house.   I also wanted to know more about this *invisible person* named God, to see if he was really *watching over us*. After attending some of the Bible study classes, I started watching biblical stories on television such as *Ben Hur,* and *King of Kings.*

After attending *Bible Study* and watching those movies, I was now having somewhat of an understanding of God. And why his son Jesus died on the Cross. I was so into the theory that Jesus died for our *SINS*, which I took my one and only *G.I. Joe toy* on *Good Friday*, wrapped it in a towel, and placed it in a drawer. I would not take it out to play with until *Easter Sunday*. This was my odd way to pay respect to the crucifixion of *Jesus on the Cross dying for Our Sins!* I thought I would sacrifice going without my *G. I. Joe* for a couple of days...I could have played with my sister's *"Barbie Dolls"* But, I knew even at my young age that I might be sending my family and my friends the *"wrong message"* about me. Who knows, next they might be worried that I might be wearing one of my sisters *Dresses* for that matter! So, I was left with no toy to play with for the weekend of Easter. And, that was fine with me.

As we continued to live in our apartment in the city of Detroit, we would have *Roaches* and *'Huge Rats'* that would pay us a visit in our apartment from time to time. The roaches, I did not care much for because they were ugly and a nuisance, but harmless *(unless you accidentally 'ate one"… because I was not aspiring to be on 'Survivor man")* There were some of the *Rats* I saw that were as big as *Cats*! I had seen the movie *Willard,* and even enjoyed the song *Ben* from the movie, but I still did not want to have them as *Pets…*

My father was a *Sharp Shooter* in the Army. He would wait with a **BB gun** for a *Rat* to *try* and enter through the water pipes behind the refrigerator.   When he would spot one of these creatures, my father would hit them right in the head with a shot! Yikes! I was always afraid of those hairy things. I am to this day afraid of anything that resembles a *Rat*! *(Later in life I would learn to also dislike the human kind of 'Rats")*

Overall, we all survived the infiltration of *Rats* and *Roaches* while growing up. Our whole family, even though we were not *Rich in Money,* we all tried to appreciate what we did have. Christmas time brought us *ONE* gift, not *TEN*. We knew how to appreciate everything we were able to afford in this household. We were very close as a family, despite our everyday struggles. While we were growing up in this tough section of Detroit, my brother's and I had to defend ourselves most every day!

We did have some other problems growing up in this area of Detroit from the neighborhood *"BULLIES,"* and especially, when attending school. One day in particular, when my brother Gary was walking over a Bridge on his way to School, he was met by some local thugs who were looking for trouble. While Gary was trying to avoid a confrontation with these youths, they chased Gary and attempted to throw him over an *Expressway Overpass*! Thank God a man yelled at the gang to leave my brother alone! The Thugs left without another attempt on Gary. The incident *Terrified* Gary, and sent a message to all of us to *Be Careful*. It was always an ongoing *Battle* for us boys to go to school *"Literally!"*

My oldest brother Mark, well, he was the

Business Minded Brother in the family. He was busy making money *Delivering Newspapers* at the early age of 12. He had once told me that his goal was to be in a better financial position in his life than what we had growing up as a family. Because we saw the downside of not being financially secure as a family. We wanted to earn some money for the extra things that we wanted as kids.

We received a daily allowance of Twenty five cents! That did not but a lot of candy and toys. We thought if we can earn some extra cash that would help take some of the financial burden off of our parents. As a young kid I would go along with my brother Mark on weekends to watch his wagon (*that he would use to haul his orders of newspapers*) while Mark would be busy delivering them to his customers. *(So no one would mistake it for "Free Press" Literally)* Mark would pay me for assisting him. I enjoyed the opportunity to earn some money of my own. *Gary* had his own outlook on how he wanted his life to be. That outlook was not very clear to Mark and me, but Gary did not want to be the center of attention in our family…

But he did have great *Drawing Skills*…Gary could draw *Detailed Pictures* of almost anything…He never pursued a Career in Art, which was a shame because Gary had a talent for it…   He enjoyed drawing pictures of *Monsters* and of his Hero *Bruce Lee*… And, if any of Gary's friends would make him angry, Gary would draw *detailed* illustrations of them getting *Gang Banged* by the *Village People*!   Gary also enjoyed watching '*Kung Fu*" movies. Gary preferred keeping to himself most of the time.   Later in life he would have numerous relationships, (*one in which would produce a Child*) but he never married.

Sadly, we would lose my brother Gary in **2003** to *Leukemia.* I (*to this day*) miss him. The conversations Gary and I would have been not always "*Pleasant",* but like in all families, siblings have their own ways of doing things. And with that, we had the common *one or two issues* with one another growing up. But in the end, Gary and I both knew we loved each other in spite of our differences! As for my sister Kathy, she and I were like *two peas in a pod!* You would rarely find us separated.

We enjoyed *Drawing Pictures* and selling them to the local Neighbors' for a *Nickel.* My sister and I knew that most of the people who bought our *Artwork* did it because they felt Sorry for us. Kathy and I would also hang around the local neighborhood Party store and buy candy from there. We also enjoyed meeting new friends to play with in the area. Kathy was beautiful, smart, and tough too! I remember Kathy defending herself against a local pair of *Twins* who lived in the same apartment complex as us, who tried to *Bully* her.   And when Kathy was finished taking on *Both Girls (at the same time!)* they looked like they just fell *on their Face* about *1000* Times!

Remember, we were all taught to be Tough! But, what Kathy loved most of all…was *Sports (any kind)* which made her a *Good Catch* for any Lucky Guy! …. *(She would later be sent to Pittsburg PA to live at age eight. more about that later…)*

Our father would always remind us kids growing up to use *Common Sense* and to keep our Eyes Open at all times. It was good information. We would always pay attention to our surroundings...*Common Sense* as he would put it; you are *Born With* not taught! One day, I learned first Hand how *Common Sense* would be my saving grace... I was about eight years old. My Parents asked me to pick-up my sister Kathy from a home of a friend across the street. It was supper time at our home. So, off I went. When I arrived at the apartment where my sister's friend lived, I was told by the father of the girl that they were not there.

But, he stated *"Let's go together and find them"* I saw nothing wrong with us going. So, he and I went to go look for Kathy and his daughter. When we first got into the Elevator, he did something that made me wary of the intentions of this man, he reached into his pocket, and handed me a "Nickel" ...I thought it was kind of *odd* for him to give me anything.   But, I met this man a few times, and thought he was just trying to be kind. So, I cautiously took it. But, he did something even odder; he pushed the *Basement button* on the Elevator?

I was now starting to get a little bit more concerned. I was thinking to myself, "Why would they be in the basement?" "It is too nice outside (**70's**) to want to play in a Basement. With that *"weird move"* we arrived in the basement. And we started looking around the area of the Basement. After looking around the basement, I determined that they were nowhere in sight. I said; "Well, I guess they are not here, I better get going"

Then, to my surprise, he *took me by the hand,* and with his other hand he began *Pulling down his zipper!* I got scared. I knew that I was in a bad situation. I wanted no part of what this Man's intentions were. I knew to get out of that basement as quickly as possible. So, I quickly *"Ripped my hand away, and ran up the stairs"* …and I mean I was running *FAST, just like Forest, Forest Gump! I would have made Jenny Proud!* Seriously though, I could not believe how fast I was running! I just had an instinct to get out of there as fast as I could. I ran straight to my home!

When I arrived home, I told my mother and father about what just happened. After explaining to my parents in detail about what I just escaped from, my mother became upset. But, my father was…Well, *MAD* as *HELL*! let's just say, *thank god my mother called the police before my father located the "BULLETS" for his Pistol*…Later when the police arrived, they asked me what happened. After I explained everything that had occurred to the officer, they went to the home where this man lived to question him.

When the police exited the father's home, I noticed the father was in *Handcuffs*! I also noticed that one side of one of the officer's face was *Red*…I was told later that when the father was being questioned by the officer about the incident, the father got angry and *"Slapped"* the officer! I guess with the attempt on me, you can also add *Assault and Battery* Charges on a police officer to the charges on this Man…

A few months later, my mother and I were to go to court. I was to testify against this man *(the court thought it would be wise to leave my Father at home, and we agreed!)*But, before the trial was to begin, the father took a *guilty plea* and he and his family agreed to go back to *INDIA* rather than face the charges against him here. I guess the man knew he was *Guilty*!

After that incident, my brothers and I continued to use our God given *Common Sense* in the neighborhood. There were some nights we would hear *popping sounds* in the neighborhood that were similar to those of Fireworks…But the *Sounds* we heard popping around here were not *Fireworks*, they were real *Gunshots*! So now, we had to keep a watchful eye around the house. Who knows, we could get Struck by a *Stray Bullet* if we were not careful…

There was also a lot of *Prostitution* going on in the area (*the other kind of "Whore"*) and because of them; you could easily mistake a *Used Condom* for a *Balloon*… Also, *Used Syringes* were always lying on the ground (*left in the area by drug users*)…So, awareness of our surroundings was a daily habit for us…And knowing our father's way of *Discipline*, staying away from Crime was in our best interests…

Chapter 2 *(Life Changing Events)*

Here is an example of some careless violence in
our neighborhood.   In the summer of *1975* when
I was *15*, our family lost a good friend **Kenny
Jones** to Violence.   He was killed with A shotgun
blast to his face (*over a drink*) He was *22*.

Kenny was a troubled person, (*Neglected by his
parents*) But, He was tough as nails. No one (*but
my father*) could put him on his ass. Kenny was
known in the area as "*TANK*". Kenny earned that
nickname for the way he would just destroy
anyone in a fight. I saw him Toss around a few
guys like a bag of grapes!

One day, Kenny wanted to show just how
tough he was to my father and some of my
father's Buddies. When Kenny started his attack,
he took down three of my father's friends in
s*econds* with his moves. But, when it was my
father's turn, Kenny *never saw the punch,* and to
our surprise, down Kenny went!   After that event,

I think Kenny had a newfound respect for my father. Still, my parents took Kenny in and treated him like he was one of the families.

 When Kenny was killed, our whole family was devastated! It was as if my parents had just lost a son, and we just lost a brother…It was a senseless act of crime. This was the first time I had to deal with a loss of someone close to me in my life. The event of Kenny's death changed me as a person.

 After this event, and while I was getting older, I wanted to grow up to be as tough as Kenny…Not a *Bully*… I wanted to be the *Protector* of my friends and family. You see, I was this *skinny kid* that was afraid of any kind of fist fight with anyone. One day in particular when I was 13, I was chased home by one of the *School Bullies*. And, not just to my home, but to my *FRONT DOOR!*

 When my Father first noticed, I was sweating and out of breath! He asked; "What is wrong with you?" I quickly explained to him that I was chased home by someone from school. My father looked at me with disgust, and yelled to me; "Get your ass out there, and beat his ass, or I am going to beat your ass". I felt so *ashamed* of myself

(*and embarrassed*) because, I looked like a
COWARD in front of my father…Well, that made
me feel worthless and ashamed of myself.

I then got this feeling of anger. And, how
pathetic I must look in the eyes of my father…I
knew my Father hated *Cowards* and I did not
want my father to see me as a *Coward*! So, I ran
out of the apartment and up the stairs as fast as I
could. I then ran up and grabbed the kid that
chased me home from the back of his hair, and
started to *beat him without remorse* until *his* father
came down from their apartment to pull me off of
him!   A few minutes passed, and I got up. I was
so excited to tell my father what I just did…

As I walked with my shoulders high into our
apartment, my father had a *Hamm's Beer* with
Two Glasses waiting for me! He must have looked
out the window and witnessed what was
unfolding. I noticed that he had this *Big Smile* on
his face. My Father then said; *"I am proud of you
Champ, let's drink-up"* We drank our glass of
Beer. Even though I did not like the taste of Beer,
I felt a sense of accomplishment at the time.

I knew in my heart that in my father's eyes…
that was the day I proved to myself, and to my

father, I was no longer a *coward*, But, that I was now a Man! Within weeks of that life changing event, I joined a local *Boxing Gym...*

The gym was Located in the local Projects. The gym was where I wanted to start practicing my *Boxing skills*, mainly because I wanted to be the best fighter in the neighborhood. Because I knew I could take a punch (*my father's*). And because of this, *I know* there was no tougher man that could deliver a *harder* blow to my head than my father.

I also wanted the security of knowing how to *properly deliver a speedy blow*! At the gym I was learning all the skills needed to become a disciplined pupil in the art of *self defense*. After a few months at the gym, I was no longer afraid of anyone! At School, I wanted to "protect" my friends who did not want to fight with *Punks* and *Bullies*. I was a lot like the *Bob Probert (Detroit Red Wings player)* of the neighborhood. My *technique* was that I would wait for the *"proper time"* to get to someone who has threatened my family or friends, and when they would least expect it, I would give them a *"Beating they would never forget!"*

Most of the bullies would later decide it was *too painful* to pick on my friends and me. So, *(after an encounter with me)* most of them became a *reformed Bully*!

But as for my mother, she was having concerns about my newfound confidence. Her main concern was that one day I would track down the person who shot our friend *Kenny*. So, my mother and father agreed to have me go visit my uncle and aunt in a suburb of Pittsburg, PA for the summer of **1975.**

They lived in a really good area of Pittsburg Called *Verona*, an area my mother thought was safe for me to stay out of trouble. My sister Kathy was sent there when she was eight, because there was an incident of a man *"exposing himself"* to young girls in our neighborhood.

My parents decided that we lived in an area of Detroit that was too dangerous to raise a Daughter…

Chapter 3 *(Learning Commitment)*

When I arrived in *Pittsburg*, I immediately noticed that My Aunt and Uncle was a *loving couple*. My Uncle (***Joe***) was a hard working Man. He was always the first one up, early in the morning to get ready for work at the *local Mill*. And he exemplified *"Hard Honest Work*! He also enjoyed adding a lot of humor to the family (*which I always looked forward to*) which made him a joy to be around…

He immediately took me under his wing and set a great foundation of simple rules to live by. He would teach me how to be responsible with the daily chores in and around their home. He stated to me; "Scott, if you fill your day up with good honest hard work, you will feel a sense of accomplishment on a daily basis!"

I liked his way of thinking, so I really wanted to have that kind of feeling. My aunt and uncle along with my sister Kathy would schedule some daily chores for me to do around their home. The first household task that my uncle taught me was cutting the grass. That was easy! *But then*, my uncle demonstrated to me how to *cut hedges.* And frankly, I think I cut more *Extension Cords* than hedges… My uncle would to *count my fingers* after I would do any hedge cutting from then on.

After my *extension cord trimmings*, my uncle thought it was *safer* for me to help my Aunt Kay with the cleaning of the inside of the home, and after these events…I agreed.

My aunt (***Katrina***)…Well there are not enough words to describe this *WONDERFUL WOMAN!* She was the *MOST Caring, Loving, Protective Mother that a Family could have.* I remember how this *"Angel" of a woman* took care of me when I first came to visit them at the age of five.

When I was visiting them at the young age of five, I remember becoming *"Deathly ill"* with a virus that eventually attacked my kidneys. My mother and father back in Michigan did not have money for health insurance. I was not covered for any doctors' visits, or medications. This left my aunt to play the role of *Doctor* and *Nurse* for me. I was amazed how this woman would carry me on her back *(because I was too weak to walk)* so that I could use the toilet…Day after day; this *"Amazing Woman"* would look after me. After a few months in her care, *amazingly* I started feeling better! But I knew, if it wasn't for her…I would have *probably died*…She was ever so determined to keep me alive. I survived…*No, she was not going to let me die…Not on her watch!* My Aunt nursed me back to health and *"never gave up"* to save me!

I was *blessed* to have her watch over me at my time of need!

While my aunt was known for her kindness to people, she was also a mother that would not take any *'Bullshit"* from any of her children, and especially from me! I think *"Judge Judy'* stole the *Copyrights* from my aunt! Because my aunt could *see right through you* if *you are* or *are not* being truthful to her in seconds! When you were to answer any of her questions, you better not lie, because she will make you look like an *"IDIOT"*….

With those *Parenting Skills,* my aunt and uncle were also heavily involved at the local *Greek Orthodox Church.* My aunt would bake her

Famous Greek Treats for *ALL* the Fundraising
events for the Church…Including for the annual
"**Greek Wine Festival**" that was sponsored by the
local church that my aunt and uncle
Attended…

The wine festival was an annual event in the
community. There was *Greek Dancing,
Souvenirs, and yes…Some of the Best food and
desserts for you to enjoy*! This *Celebration* is still
held every year in *June*. I recall people would
come from miles around to this wonderful three
day event! I really enjoyed my stay in Pittsburg
with my aunt and uncle. All this made for some
great times around these fantastic relatives for
someone like me who was raised in the *down and
out* area of Detroit! Along with their belief in
GOD, and their good Community work, my aunt
and uncle also had three children of their own.

The oldest was a Girl *(Sarah)* she was not only
Beautiful, but classy! She was never influenced
by anybody, mainly because she was raised by her
parents to *respect herself first* along with
respecting others…Sarah was known in the area
for how well she carried herself *(so the boys in the
area that were up to "no good" knew to look*

elsewhere..) Sarah eventually married a great
man. He was a great husband and father to their 3
kids!

Then there was the only Son *(George).* He
also had the same values as Sarah, and all that any
parent would want in a son. He took a position as
a *High School Teacher*, and was a Great example
for the future college attendees. George also
worked at the local church with his father. He and
his Beautiful *and Smart* wife **Christine** would
invite Kathy and me over to swim during my stay.
George was also *like a Brother* to me. He made a
good life for him and his family because of his
"Choices" in life.

I remember asking him about life, and he
would offer some suggestions about building a
good life for Me. George was not only good
looking, but he had a great personality to boot! I
asked him how I could meet a woman as good as
his wife (Christine). He stated; "Scott, there are
Sluts and *Whores* that you play with, and then
there are the women that have more to offer in a
relationship that you marry".
He added; "Christine is the *Total Package!"*

I was in alliance with those words. I did not

want to marry *a slut or a Whore,* so I kept that *very important* information in my head. Later in their marriage, while George and Christine tried for years to have a baby, they figured it was now time to adopt. And they adopted a beautiful baby boy named *Nathan.* Later that same year, Christine was blessed to find out that she was Pregnant! Yes ironically, after adopting a child, they were finally blessed with a child of their own...A little Girl Named *Jasmine*!

Finally, there was the youngest (***Kerri***) She was a *nature lover*...She loved all that nature provided...Kerri would only use items that were without all the harmful chemicals and preservatives that pollute this world...And Kerri rarely used any make-up...Well, the fact is, Kerri did not have to, she had what most woman wanted, and that was *Natural Beauty!* Kerri later met a wonderful man named *Nick* whom she married. Nick is a wonderful husband and father of their two kids...

A little about my half *Brother George.* He was staying with my mother's sister (***Stefanie***) and her husband (***Greg***). They raised George with the same values that my aunt and uncle did. George was a *ladies' man,* but had the utmost respect for his *"Parents"* that any mother and father could ask for. He also had three other siblings he was raised with, and loved them as *Brothers* also. My brother George would eventually marry, and have two *'Beautiful and Exceptionally Gifted Athletic"* daughters of his own. Yes he was blessed!

Now that I covered most of our relatives in PA *(because there are many more to talk about, if I was writing three books!)*, let's just get back to my Aunt and Uncle....They were a *"GOD Fearing"* family.....And because of those beliefs, it added -up to a great life for themselves... *they had it all...A Nice home in a suburb, a ton of friends, and...they were "Happily Married" for many years!* Yes, they had their disagreements, but at the end of the day, they always expressed to each other their *"Committed Love"* ...

My parents raised us differently, to be tough and aware of our surroundings! As for my Aunt and Uncle, they raised their family in a different culture...And with their guidance; they were a great example for me on how wonderful life could be if you are *committed to God First!* Furthermore, because of how they lived, I witnessed how GOD really provided for them! I thought, O.k., so how can I achieve this?

I asked my Aunt and Uncle to help me develop more of an understanding on how to make a great life for myself and eventually for a family of my own someday. First thing on their agenda, was for me to get involved with the local *Greek Orthodox Church* that they were heavily involved in. My aunt and Uncle stated that *"I needed to understand the meaning of Love and commitment, along with the purpose of life, so I could provide a great life for myself and a family someday"*

With their guidance, I took on the responsibility of becoming an *"Alter Boy"* *(No jokes here, we were Orthodox, Not Catholic!)* It was a challenge *(getting up so early on Sunday)*. But, I did enjoy the role of Altar Boy...I remember loving the smell of the *incense* that was a part of the role of this position on Sunday mornings. I also enjoyed the *Readings* from the Bible by the priest...

Our priest *(Father Rick)* after his Sunday services would go from home to home to stay in touch with the local families. And provide any remedy of the Lord's guidance if needed...He did not wear all the *"Glitter"* as some priests wear today. But, the knowledge and Power of GOD that he did have on the *"inside"* I believe is worth more than SILVER and *GOLD*…Combine all this, now I am starting to have a sense of a *Different kind of Strength*! Not the feeling you get from lifting weights, but this feeling was of love, and of God's Presence in my life. It was like a *warm feeling* in my stomach….And now with this new *Epiphany,* I felt like I wanted to be <u>*a man of GOD, and*</u> with this newfound faith in God, I wanted to serve a *good purpose* on this planet. With his blessings and, as I continued my role as altar boy at the church, I knew I was also making my Aunt and Uncle proud of me. *(Later, in this Story…I will also "Disappoint them")*

I also had a better understanding about life and what Commitment it takes to become a man of *God.* But while I was there, I still had some of the *"Detroit boy"* in me. With that, I protected over my sister *Kathy*. She was a Beautiful girl now at age **14**. I thought she was the *Lucky* one of us to live under the guidance of my Aunt and Uncle… And while I was there some of the local guys that thought that they would *"TRY"* to take advantage of her.

I was thankfully there just to let them know what kind of Son my father has raised in Detroit. I was my Father's Son, and I was given that *GIFT,* So why not spread ... *"My Love Around"...LOL...Kathy would later marry a guy who cared more about himself than her, and they later divorced.*

After three summers serving as an altar boy in Pennsylvania, and receiving more of the knowledge and understanding of what a bright future could be in store for me.
I was ready to head back to Detroit.

What I had just learned from these *"Two Wonderful People"* (*my aunt and uncle*) was the meaning of *love* and *Commitment* in a relationship. To understand how to maintain a healthy Marriage and to provide for a family, also essential to a good life, is to have the guidance of GOD in all my decisions. I felt that living with these principles, it will enable me to provide for a family of my own someday!

Yes, my aunt and uncle ...they *were my Role Models*....And my friend, that was exactly what I needed. Although I respected and loved my

parents, I also needed the influence of my aunt
and uncle to give me the *Proper Tools* of living
life the proper way! I really felt in my heart that
my Aunt and Uncle really cared about my future.
I do not mean this in a bad way; I kind of wished
that they were my *parents*. The reason I state this
is because of the positive impact they had on me
while I was there.

I witnessed first- hand how they really had
their *priorities* in line …*God first*, and then come
Family and everything else! I was grateful for the
great experience I gained from spending time with
my aunt and uncle. I remember *crying* while
traveling on the Greyhound Bus back home to
Michigan, because of how much I was going to
"Love and Miss" their company.

I returned back home to *Michigan*, not as an
angry man, but as a more *complete man.* Now I
felt as if I was a *Man of God*…And, I was on a
Mission…A Mission to better my life!…To live
my life with the Ten Laws that GOD gave to
Moses. *(The Ten Commandments) W*ith the
knowledge that I gained from my aunt and uncle,
the first thing in my *"Pursuit of Happiness"* Was
that I wanted to land a good job.

And along the way to my goals, I wanted to stay away from trouble! My goal was to pursue a career in the food industry. My father was a *Great Cook.* My Father would take a pack of *"Neck Bones" (Sorry, only us Poor People know what those are)* and make a *five star* meal out of them. Also on my agenda, I wanted to find the *"Woman of my Dreams" (Not a slut, or a Whore to play with as my cousin George warned me)...* Nope! Good women, the "Total Package" as he said, get married, and hopefully start a family of my own. I also wanted to join a local church to attend. *(Just like my aunt and uncle.)*

*Wait though...A little back in my story...*During my stay in PA, I got a call from my mother, and informed me that my older brother (Mark) was jumped and beaten by a handful of *local gang members* in Detroit. Mark was in the hospital over-night because of the injuries he sustained. Even though I was steering away from trouble, I wanted to see if God would put at least one of them in my path... And <u>*HE DID!*</u>

It was a nice and cool Summer Evening. I was driving my 1973 Dodge Dart down *Cass* Ave in Detroit, when I noticed a familiar *"PUNK"* riding his *Ten Speed Bike* to a Stop light. As I got closer to take a look at this guy, I noticed he was one of the guys that jumped my older brother Mark. I started to feel my heart rate increasing, I was also "biting my lower lip" and "grinding my teeth" just eager to get to this *"Punk"*… I then placed my car in the park position as fast as I could, and I ran over to this guy. When I reached him; he had this look of surprise on his face.

Then quickly I *"knocked this Thug off of his bike"*…and, I took the knit cap that he was wearing on his head, and wrapped it around my hand *for protection of my knuckles*. I proceeded to *"Pound"* his face as hard as I could! As I was doing *my version* of an *Extreme Makeover* to his face, he cried out; *'who are you?"* I answered back between punches with these *"sweet whispers"* in his now bloody ears. *"The youngest Longas Brother"*

After I had completed turning his face into *a Ground Beef Special,* I went over to his Bike, and *'bent the front wheel"* so the thug could now *drag himself to the hospital*! I then hurried back to my car and drove off!   I then felt…Well, let's just say that my *"Vital Signs"* were now normal! I felt this was *REAL* justice! Make no mistake here; it was not that my older brother Mark could not have done the same; I was just the *first one* to get to this "*COWARD*" who jumped him! (*As for "turning the other cheek" well, I thought this did not apply, I took it as if I was a "TOOL" in doing God's good work!*)

After this event, a few years later Mark would end up falling in love and married a *Local Greek Woman* who was a few years older than him. And, to this day are still married.

But sadly, after numerous attempts to have a Child (*miscarriages*) they still remained *Strong in their faith in God...*
Do not place blame on God for their misfortune.
It is a shame though, because I know they would have been
"*Wonderful Parents*" to any lucky child!

Chapter 4 *(the "Meeting")*

In my continued pursuit for a better life for myself, In **1978** I took a Position at a *local Sports Bar* known for its Great Hamburgers. It was also a popular place for local sports professionals and Celebrities to gather for a drink and a burger.

I worked for the two *Greek Brothers* who owned the place…One of the brothers ran the Day shift and was the *"Business Minded One"*… The other brother worked the Night shift and was the *"Celebrity"* of the Bar. They were both small in stature, but would pack a *"Big man's Punch"* if you crossed them! The night shift Brother was known for his *"Brass Knuckle Punch"*. He would make many men *go to sleep in an instant* with that piece of hardware!

With that technique, most of the patrons were warned to behave……I got into a few *"scraps"* myself while I was there.

It was because *"they started it"*… as I would tell my friend (*Tommy*) that work at the bar with me at the time. Tommy would know better though, he would always tell me to *"stay out of tut-tut (trouble) But, only as he would say it to me*...My position at the Bar was the *Dayshift bartender*. It was an exciting position...I would serve the local *Michigan Bell* employees their drink of choice.

I also enjoyed the chance to develop my "People Skills" during my tenure there......I was a *Tough looking Guy* (*looks compared to a Robert Deniro, as most of my friends would say*) tough yes, but only if you were up to no good. Otherwise, if your intentions were good, I was known to be a *likeable person*.

I was also a good listener. I wanted *everyone to like me* despite my angry looks...As I worked the day shift at the bar; I tried to please most everyone. And yes, sometimes I would have to be brutally honest with some of the patrons. I think that was the reason why they enjoyed conversations with me.

While I was employed there, I would meet the likes of: *Billy Martin, Sonny Elliott,* and even *Mickey Mantle!* The Bar was also a Popular Place to meet Women. Yes, I met and dated a few of the regulars...

But, none of them were even close to the "*Woman of my dreams*" that I was looking for. They were the *Sluts* and *Whores* that I was told to "Stay away from".

Then one day after coming back from the *Boxing Gym*, I stop off at the local neighborhood pub for a drink with some of my friends. And, like a "*Bolt of lightning*" I saw "*the Most Beautiful Woman*" that I have ever seen in my life. She looked like a Famous singer named *Laura Branigan.* She was "*Stunning*"! *Long dark hair, tall, long legs and with a Beautiful smile.* I knew I just had to meet her.

I first noticed that she seemed out of place in "*my run down part of the neighborhood*". I was wondering what the hell she was doing in this *dangerous part of the city*…So, after asking around the bar about this Woman, I learned that she was visiting a local friend of hers in the area.

After finding out who this person was, I asked the local girl whom she was meeting some questions about this "Beautiful Woman". I came to learn that this woman's name was "***Heather***" from a local suburb. So with the help of the local girl, a meeting was set-up with Heather and me.

When I first got the chance to finally meet with Heather, we sat down for a drink and some conversation. (*My heart was beating as if it was about to jump out of my chest!*)After getting to know more about Heather and her Family, I asked Heather for her phone number so I could see her again.

She was a little hesitant to provide it for me (*Turned out she was seeing the local girl's brother*) But I did not care; I insisted that she give me her number. In addition, I said "*you got to go out with me*" With a little hesitation, Heather gave me her phone number. I was *elated!* I said to myself, "*Thank-You* God" I am now going on a date with a woman that quite possibly could be... the "Woman of my Dreams". I felt like God has sent her especially for me in this "SHITHOLE" of a neighborhood. I was starting to feel like the luckiest man alive!

I knew before I was able to see her exclusively, I would have to remove a certain "PUNK" from the scene! I had to stop the Ex-boyfriend from harassing, and threatening her.

One day while I was visiting Heather at her home, her Ex called. I just happened to be there, so I answered her phone…His conversation started by making threats against Heather, stating he was going to come over to Heather's home with his 'Biker Buddies" and Rape her! If that wasn't enough for me to get angry, this Idiot then added ME to his list of threats…

After the "Telephone Tough Guy" completed telling me his Christmas card wish list for Santa, I hung up the phone! I waited at Heather's home for him and his buddies to show up. After the "Coward" did not follow through on the Threat, I called him. I arranged a meeting with his older brother *(you see, this EX of Heather's was too small for me to fight, so I wanted to take it out on his older brother)*

The next day, the older brother of this thug and I met to fight. And while we were fighting, I noticed from my left side that Heather's Ex was coming towards me with a **2x4**! As I glanced over, wouldn't you know it…I got hit to the side of my head by the EX'S older brother! And, down I went… Thank GOD my older brother Gary was there. Gary and another friend started hammering the older Brother for what he did. And after I cleared the "Butterflies from my head", I started running after Heather's punk ex-boyfriend......Well; I was not so clearheaded to catch the little "Coward"... So, he got away... But I did eventually go back and helped finish off (beat, not KILL) the older brother....

After that incident; her EX would never bother Heather again! After that encounter, it was time to finally go out with Heather...

And when I arrived at Heather's home to pick her up, to my surprise, her "Entire Family" was there to greet me!   There was: Her Father (**Vito**) He was a first generation Italian Immigrant. I would eventually learn to have a lot of respect for this man, because not only did he speak "very limited" English, but when he arrived here from Italy, he had only fifteen **(15) dollars** in his pocket! But yet, he managed to work past those limitations to provide a wealthy lifestyle for his wife and kids.

Heather's father was a City worker, but it was his "Hard Work" that this man was known for. Along with making an income for his family, He would always take time out of his busy schedule to help others who might have needed any kind of assistance.   Or if they needed a real friend to give them any kind of support.

Heather's father had also taught me how to play a Card game that was a household favorite in any Italian home. The card game was called 'Scoba". After learning this fun game, we would all enjoy passing some time playing this fun game with Heather's family. He worked hard and always provided for his family. I noticed how he was a very devoted husband and father (*similar to my Aunt and Uncle*). This made me feel lucky to meet him.

Heather's Mother (*Angelina*) was also a first generation Italian. I realized that she caught on to the English language much faster than her husband. She was the "ANGEL" in this family...She was the Chief Cook, and anything that needed attention person in the family...What a Saint she was...*(More about this 'Great Woman' later in the story...)*

Then there was Heather's Brother (**Rocco**), He was the promising young Doctor in the family. He was gifted as a doctor. Because of his skills, he was selected as the team Doctor for the San Francisco 49ers during the year they won the "Super Bowl" in **1982**(*Pontiac silver dome*) He also was the "Final approval" person in the family.   He the one to go to before anyone in their family made any Big Decisions. Why you may ask? Well, because he was the only one in their family who had a College education… Also, he was in the "Top Five in his class" at Med School. So, I say…Why not?

As for his wife **Kerri,** She was a wonderful person. She was very supportive of her husband, with his goals to be a Great Doctor. Kerri would work to support the family while her husband was going through grueling Medical School requirements. Rocco worked long hours building his successful medical practice (*where Heather worked as his office manager*), while making sure he could provide a good life for his wife and family.   Rocco and I "hit it off" pretty quickly when we first met. He and I could almost pass for 'Brothers" (*but, I was better looking…LOL*) But we would enjoy our conversations about family, work, and life during family gatherings.

I admired his life accomplishments. He was a Great Doctor, well respected by all, and he NEVER lacked confidence in me, even when I lacked it in myself! Throughout our relationship, we both learned to respect each other as men. I would always want to be there for him if he needed me, as he would for me as well. (I would eventually disappoint this great man too)

Heather's Sister (**Anna**) she worked as a Home Specialist. Her husband (**Joe**) worked as a Builder. They would welcome everyone with a Smile! And along with it, some Great "ITALIAN" Food!

Joe was a hard working man. He had some "English limitations", but he was as intelligent as they come. He knew more about this country's history than some "Self proclaimed professors" He was a Soccer Fan, and watching those games with him gave me a new respect for the sport of Soccer. (No "Overweight players" in that sport!)

Joe and Anna were wonderful parents to their two Daughters…

Then, you add all of her nieces and nephews that were also there… I thought, Wow, she must be someone special in their lives for all of them to be here on our first date.

I am feeling like a "lucky man" to have the opportunity to date her. After meeting her 'Entire Family"…

Heather and I went to a movie on our first date. We had a great time! And, to my surprise… there was "No Sex Talk" which is what I really respected about her.

And as far as our First Kiss ….Well, it was "Magical"…Because after our first Kiss… I knew this had to be "THE ONE" for me! I was thankful that she was a "Real Lady" not like the "Drop your panties" on the first date kind of women I was accustomed to…

Nope, Heather was "ALL CLASS! Heather was just the type of woman my cousin George in Pittsburg found in Christine… I remember after our date that evening, that I could still smell Heathers perfume scent still on my shirt when I arrived home… (*Which I still remember to this day*)

I really enjoyed my evening with Heather. I was really into this Woman….I thought, I do not have a lot of Money, or Fame…But Heather and I really enjoyed each other's company, no matter what our 'Status" in life was…Because I did not need a House in Beverly Hills, or a Vacation Home in Cancun to have a relationship with Heather…

No, I came to learn during our first date that Heather's Goals were the same as mine. And that was to fall in love, build a Future together with someone "Special"...And hopefully marry, and raise a family!

After Heather and I enjoyed our first date with the promise of possibly building a relationship together, we agreed to continue dating, and to see where our relationship goes from there...

After our first date, Heather and I started going out on a regular basis. Over the next year and a half, I fell in love with Heather and her family. My parents, along with my siblings also fell in love with this 'Great Woman" that I have been dating...

Now here is the final test for us, I wanted the approval from some great people who provided me with the foundation I needed as a young man. So, Heather and I took a trip to Pittsburg PA., to meet My Aunt Katrina, and my Uncle Joe and their family!

I was eager to take Heather there, and wanted my aunt and uncle to meet this 'Amazing Woman" in my life!

After my aunt and uncle had the chance to

meet and get to know all about Heather and her family, they pulled me aside and stated; "That Woman is Someone Special" and added; To "Always respect her (*if we were to marry*) and, to continue living by the rules of God in my life". I reassured them that I would...

After our visit to meet my Aunt and Uncle, I returned home with the sense of "Determination" not to lose this 'Wonderful Woman" in my life! I began to show how 'Big" my love was for this woman. I would buy Heather some great big "Stuffed Animals" to show my love and affection for her. I would leave this life like animal at her door, and ring the doorbell for Heather to answer. I thought it was kind of romantic, but I gave these "BIG" gifts to Heather to show how 'BIG" my love was growing for her...

After I continued coming over to spend more time with Heather and her family, I felt as though I was becoming a member of Heather's family. I remember eating dinner with her family almost every night. It was as if God picked this special woman to come into my life. In addition, he rewarded me with her Great Family, who accepted me as one of their own. I was on cloud nine!

Chapter 5   ("Commitment")

So now after a year and a half, I was ready to take our relationship further.

After first asking her parents' permission, I popped the "Big question" to Heather..."Will you marry me" Heather said "yes" And, I was Ecstatic!   *(I think I had to change my underwear!)*

Right then I thought..."Scott, you are the luckiest man on the face of the earth!" Heather and I started making plans to get married the following year.

On **AUGUST 29 1981,** Heather and I were married! I was so happy! In addition, let me explain about this wedding, it was the "Wedding of the Century"...We had close to **400** guests. We also enjoyed some excellent food, Entertainment, Even a **12**-foot dessert table with two white doves, and the violinist from the movie "the Godfather" played at OUR ceremony.

And, for a midnight appetizer......Two **STUFFED PIGS!**

In my mind, it compared to Princess Diana's

wedding held that same year. Her parents covered all the expenses. It must have been at least **$25,000**. Today a wedding like that would cost as much as **$100,000!**

My family and I would never forget an experience like that. Well, so I thought ... (*you will soon learn how I did forget all this and more*) Read on...

So after the wedding, Heather and I went for a two week honeymoon, and we went to California, and finally to Las Vegas! We had a great time there. We visited Knott berry Farm, and Universal Studios while in California... we continued to our destination to Las Vegas. While in Vegas, we stayed at the Dunes Hotel. We enjoyed all the Glamour and Lights that made Las Vegas the Number one destination spot in the World! After our honeymoon, Heather and I decided to move into her parent's home (*this was so we could save our money for a house of our own*) and what a treat it was to live there...

Heather's mother and father were "hard working people" They also solidified the fact that the most important thing in life was...'Family!"

While living at Heather's parents' home,

Heather's parents would go to the local farm and bring home the "Freshest' meals possible and cook them...And by that I mean..."fresh" as in "Live animals"....Yes folks, they would bring home live goats, lambs, and even "Live chickens"...

One day, they had me go to their car to grab a bag out of the car trunk. As I reached inside, I felt the bag "move" and I heard a loud "QUACK"...I came to realize that the bag was full of "live chickens".... I *pooped my pants*! They both laughed, as did Heather. So, I pretended that all was fine...I then went inside to change my underwear...

But there was always great food put on the table by Heather's parents for all of us to enjoy. Heather's parents also had a 'Huge" Vegetable garden that they would prepare and oversee every year.

The garden was so big that they could have had their own farmers market if they chose to. Neighbors would come over to "Borrow" some of the fresh vegetables from their garden because of how tasty the vegetables were....

And when it came to the Holidays?

Well…let's just say, all the relatives came over to Heather's parents home first so they could enjoy a "Great Feast" all the while we could all enjoy the Holidays together. Even the neighbors would "invite" themselves over to enjoy the great meals that Heather's parents would prepare…

Yes; living with Heather's Parents was a special place to be. All the while, we were saving money for a new home of our own… While life is going well living with Heather and her family, I would suffer a "Huge loss'…In **1983**.

Unexpectedly, my father passed away in his sleep. I was numb! He was only **56.** I was not ready for this. No one in our family ever knew he was sick. We would later learn from his doctor that he had been suffering from Heart Disease caused by his abuse of alcohol. I now had to deal with the fact that my father, who taught me how to be a man, was gone.

I remember my father always telling me I could do anything, if only I believed in it! He was also my biggest Fan. I remember when he would brag to his friends how proud he was of me when he would come watch me fight at the Local gym. He would have tears in his eyes after watching me fight. I would ask him; "Dad, why are you crying? I did not get beat-up in there". My father responded; "No you did not get beat up, but you made me feel proud watching you in that boxing ring" I knew what he meant…Now with his passing, I knew that I could no longer have him here with me in person. But I believe in GOD. And I know he will be here with me in Spirit. Therefore, even though I knew he will always be near in spirit, I would still cry for days missing my Father and "best friend" … But, as he would want me to, I had to move on and focus on my own family. Therefore, I continued to remember my father who instilled toughness and strength in my life...

Chapter 6 (My "Little girl" is born)

After the loss of my father, I Left the Sports Bar for a position at a Popular Pizza Company. The company had Great pay and benefits, along with the potential for long term success.

The owner, his wife, and family of this "Pizza Giant" built this company like "Caesar" built Rome…Along with becoming one of the most recognized pizza companies in the world, they also were instrumental in the building of Detroit's inner city. They wanted to bring back to respectability to this great city of Detroit with their local charity work, and local investments.

I was "LUCKY to have a position with this company. And in doing so, I was learning the tools of how to operate a successful business. And while under the leadership of this man and his family, I was also in the hope that someday I might have an opportunity to own a business for myself.

And with the tools of the business world that this company has given me, maybe someday I would achieve with the same hard work that they exemplified, become almost as successful as this man.

While I continued working for this Great Pizza Company, I met a "FRIEND" whom worked in the Franchise Department of this Pizza Company. His name was **Robert.** Robert would always offer words of encouragement to me when things got hectic in my life (balancing work and home)He would always tell me to "Hang in their Kid" like he knew that things might be a little hard for me to do so at the time. I will forever be indebted to Robert for his words of encouragement!

Yes, I have a lot of mentors and a great support group in my life. While Heather and I are busy with our careers, the birth of one of our friend's Daughter (*Laurie*) occurred.

The Father (*Bart*) of this precious bundle of joy was a Funny Guy. And under the watchful eye of his wife (*Sandra*) he became a good husband, and a great father! Heather met Sandra at work. Sandra was a fine woman.

Heather and Sandra were very close friends. There were some nights at Sandra and Bart's home that all four of us were up until the "wee early morning" hours playing "euchre". We did not care what time it was…Because, those times were "priceless!"

Sandra also made the best 'Rice Pilaf" in town! This was the 'Tastiest meal" on the Planet. This dish was a meal in itself! Bart and Sandra were great friends to know. Heather and I were blessed to have her and her husband as our Friends……
After visiting Bart and Sandra and their new Baby, I asked Heather "now that they had a child, when is it "our turn?"… I begged "Please Heather, I think it is time for us to have a child of our own"…Heather paused, and with this big smile Heather said "yes" …That evening when Heather and I arrived home, we were in the "making baby mode!" And if you ask me, I know that night my child was conceived! LOL…A few months later…Heather and I got the Great news that she was pregnant.   We were sooooo excited, and well, as for me…I was "OVERJOYED"
Now I am starting to put things into perspective…
I am anxiously awaiting another one of God's blessings, a Child! Man o' man, I was so grateful for this opportunity! And now, the moment of the birth of our child is arriving. So, Heather's mother

and I rush to get Heather to the Hospital.

And while Heather was in labor, Heather asked me this strange question; …"Scott, are you O.k.?"… (*Heather was thinking I might pass out from excitement*) I replied to her I was just fine. But is she worrying about me I thought? How about that, She's asking me if I was alright? (*What a tough woman Heather is*)…Worrying if I am O.K., meanwhile she is squeezing out a Baby from an area that did not look big enough for Childbirth!

As Heather is pushing, out comes the head. And as our baby was completely out, I Noticed that I was now the father of a precious little girl…. I was Numb! Yes, On **October 26 1986, at 4:50am** in the morning, Our "Wonderful Blessing" was born. That 'blessing" of a baby was an **8 lb, 10 oz** "little Girl"… We named her **"Christina".**

I then proudly cut the cord. And I was excited! And, I was so proud of Heather. Heather delivered our new Daughter without any medication. She was so tough! Heather never once screamed or complained. I was so impressed with Heather. Watching her give birth to our baby was one of the most amazing events in my life…

After this great accomplishment, I was looking forward to fatherhood with our new baby girl. When I arrived home after watching the birth of our child, I could not sleep! I thought, "Now I am a father of a beautiful baby girl, and my goals are right on track, and that the only thing left is to continue to provide for Heather and our baby Christina.

And finally, later in the week, Heather and our new baby girl were released from the hospital. We now continued to live at Heather's parent's home with our new baby daughter, and their new granddaughter Christina. Heather had recovered nicely after the birth of Christina.

So we both continued to work and save "EVERYTHING' we earned for the next **Six** years…After living with my wife's Parents for **Six** years, I was promoted to a multi-unit supervisor with a great raise and bonuses!…and soon….Our dream of homeownership will finally come upon us.

In **1988**, With a Nice Gift from Heather's Parent's of **$25,000**(*which was not expected,)* we were able to put down a large down payment on our first home (*in the city of Novi, Mi*.) We were able to get a wonderful price for the home because Heather's sister was involved with the sale of the home. We purchased a beautiful two-story home with all the amenities. And, in a Great neighborhood, with…"Sidewalks" Nope, No Rats or Roaches for my family… Now, I am feeling truly blessed! I thought that life was really shaping up for us. I was thankful for all that God was providing for us.

We also got involved with a local catholic church in the area. I joined the choir. I thought that since I enjoyed listening to *ELVIS* as a child, I thought that I could sing a little *(I thought GOD would not mind the effort I gave)* and with that, I thought I was accomplishing the Mirror life that my aunt and uncle were setting as a example for me…Yes, I was feeling the sense of accomplishment. While Heather and I were raising our family, we noticed our daughter Christina was growing up to be a smart little Girl!

For example; one afternoon when Christina was **3** years old, (*And dad was napping*) she tried to 'Self -train" herself on the proper way to "Polish the Kitchen counters" with a wonderful color of "Pink fingernail polish!" Yes, the pleasure was all mine to clean-up my daughter's newfound talent! And, before her mother (*the boss*) came home…

But I could not get rid of that *smell* of *fingernail polish*…But, who could hide that smell! When Christina was about the same age, one day (*while dad was again napping*) Christina unlatched the front door and went to the neighbors' home to play with their Dog. Yes, I got my 'wake-up call" from the neighbors telling me to get my little one…I had to "add a latch" to the front door. So, that dad could nap before work!

My little Christina was my life…I wanted to protect her from anything that could hurt my little girl! She was **"DADDY'S GIRL"**…

There was a song that would play on the radio from time to time that was pretty popular called **"Butterfly Kisses"**
(*A song about a father's little girl growing up before his eyes. And recounting all the 'Butterfly Kisses" that his daughter would give to him through the phases of her life. The song continues all the way to letting go of his "Little Girl" to*

marriage. He sang that he ALWAYS remembered the 'Butterfly Kisses" from his daughter)

Every time that song would be playing on the radio, I would "CRY"…Christina knew this. So, when the song would play on the radio, Christina would look "to see if I was crying"….The song is so true, and I never wanted to lose my little girl! *(But, you will see how I managed just that, later in this story.)*

I was '**Very Protective**" of my Christina. There was a family nearby with some 'family issues' who once threaten my daughter while she was playing in our yard…Heather and Christina told me about the incident, and I went over to the home to talk to the father. I "Nicely' asked him to "Talk" to his kids about their language towards my daughter. And if he could have his kids stop, I would come back and do my "Own Talking', No, not with his Kids, but to him! Needless to say, it stopped!

Anyway, while Christina continued growing older, I made sure she got the "Best of everything" you name it…Concert tickets, clothes, jewelry, toys, Beanie Babies(*she had so many Beanie Babies, we almost had to add an addition to our home for them all*)…I even provided "Limousine Rides" for her and her friends! Yes, my little girl had anything she wanted…

I was like Heather stated; "Wrapped around Christina's finger" And Heather was right! While our families were now forming to each other, we are all spending fun B-days and holidays together. (*They were some long all -Nighters' at times*), we would also go as a family on some Vacation trips.

Almost every year we would go with my wife's brother and his entire Medical Practice along with spouses to local Ski resorts!   While we were there, we would all get a little 'Tanked' with alcohol…Overall; we had some great fun on those trips!

Chapter 7 ("Huge" family loss)

But sadly, in **1989**, Heather's mother was stricken by a stroke that left her speechless and without eyesight. It was a terrible blow to the entire family.

I could not help but to think back to the time when my mother in law nursed me back to health from a bout of the flu in a matter of hours. She gave me a 'Hot Toddy", covered me with blankets, and told me to lie in front of the fireplace to sweat-out the sickness. Amazingly, I recovered in a *Matter of Hours...*

She was wonderful then, and I desperately wanted to help her now. Unfortunately, I could not do anything. We were heartbroken! We were all believers in God so we all prayed for a *Miracle....*

Meanwhile; my mother in law was placed in a local nursing home to hopefully recover. Unfortunately, her condition stayed the same for over a year. Some additional *sad news* came to us later that year concerning Heather's Father. He was diagnosed with Terminal Lung Cancer. What now I thought? Our faith is now being tested...We were now faced with the thought of losing both of Heather's parents. We tried to hold it together, especially for all the grandchildren's sake.

In the spring of **1992**, we received the news we all feared would come someday…My mother in law passed away. We were all saddened. Though we all knew she was not enjoying her life as she did before the stroke. And we all knew she was now in a better place, with God. She was no longer suffering. But still, her passing left a terrible void in the family.

Then, as you most often hear about when one partner passes the other follows, well, just **30** days later, Heather's father succumbed to cancer. Our Family was devastated! The two Pillars of Heather's family was gone in **30** days! This was too ironic! We were all in a state of Shock! Their passing left a huge void in the family. How can you recover from losing both your parents in almost **30** days?   But, we all managed to get through the Shock of it all…

And with the Lord's guidance; we would learn to accept the loss of these great people. After we laid them to rest, we all got closer. We all tried to carry on the family traditions and the holiday celebrations. That was what her parents would have wanted us to do. But, we all knew that life would never be the same without them!

Chapter 8 (Open for Business)

After more than year from our family's loss….Life slowly returned back to almost as normal could be. And that was for us to continue working hard, and raising our daughter.

Soon after, there was a new Strip Mall going up in our area. The location looked to be perfect for a Deli or some sort of carry-out. Heather and I discussed the possibility of opening a little carry-out shop in that new Plaza. A Restaurant of our own!

We talked about a possible carry-out Italian restaurant with fresh homemade recipes and Italian décor in memory of her parents. After writing out a Business Plan, we negotiated with the landlord with terms of a lease for the business.

After waiting for final approval of the space from the Landlord, 'IT HAPPENED"…Heather and I were scheduling to open our carryout Restaurant in December of **1993.**

We were now blessed with the opportunity of owning our own business! We were able to fund the restaurant with some of our savings, and a

Loan from our Local Bank. The Restaurant had a large variety of Italian dishes. I was the "Operator" of the Business; Heather was to be the "Secretary" which worked out for us both. On **December 29th 1993** we opened our Restaurant.

And Customers came from all areas of town to sample our food. There was a large variety of *Italian* meals to choose from. There was your staple meal of Spaghetti with meatballs, along with other Italian favorites such as lasagna, ravioli, and Chicken parmesan.

There was also a *unique* pasta and chicken dish that was added to the menu in late **1996** named the *"Explosion" that became a local favorite, and eventually was a whopping 82% of the restaurants' sales!* We also had Local sports athletes and local celebrities coming in for their weekly *"Explosion"* fix. We also had the "STANLEY CUP" visit our place of Business…Yes, business was going very well at the time. While I was working as a Chef in the area, I would also have a drawing held every month where a local family could win A *FREE NIGHT* with a *Chef* to come to their home and prepare a meal for a group of six people. And because of this, I was also able to do some side work for some extra income for our family.

We also hosted a yearly traditional Pasta eating contest to raise money for the **MAKE-A-WISH FOUNDATION** (*A charity close to my heart, that grants wishes for terminally ill children*) mainly because, I had a weakness for ALL Children! Also because of the fact that Heather and I were blessed with our healthy daughter. We also knew that GOD would want us to give back to the community…Because I believe that God was the one who blessed us with the Business, and enabled us to help this great cause.

Here I am, I have a "Wonderful Life" so far... I have a loving wife, a Beautiful Daughter, and now a Business.
Life again cannot get any better than this!

Then on **July, 11 1995**, I suffered the loss of my mother who succumbed to Heart Disease…She was a tough woman thru her illness. There were many times through the years that we thought we would lose my mother to Heart disease any day! Anyway, her death was not a surprise to us. Even though her Heart finally gave out, my mother always gave her heart to so many people!

I remember one time when my mother was visiting her sister in Pittsburgh; my mother received a new 'Winter Coat" from her sister. When my mother arrived home after traveling on the Greyhound bus, She noticed a woman whom was walking around with 'Barely any clothes on"…Well, my mother took off the 'New Coat" that she was wearing at the time and 'Gave it to the almost naked woman"!

When we arrived to take my mother home from the Bus station, we asked her; "Mom, what happened to your coat" She calmly stated; "That poor woman over there needed it more than I did, so I gave it to her"…When we looked over to see who my mother gave her coat to, we noticed that the woman was a "Known Drug Addict' from the area…But, that did not matter to my mother; she would look out for other people rather than herself! And now, the lord has another 'Angel" in his arms!

After another loss in the family, we always knew how to remember the love ones that we have lost, and with our belief in God, learned to continue our lives…But, overall everything in my Life is going well. Now, all relationships have its Fair share of Issues, with ours it was "intimacy" *This is one of the "SYMPTOMS" that ALL couples should be aware of!*

My wife and I were so busy with raising a daughter, and dealing with the loss of her parents. While both of us are working long hours, we rarely had a chance to spend time with just the TWO OF US!

But, during one of those *rare* intimate occasions… Heather became pregnant with our soon to be Second Baby. And the first few months, she was doing fine.

Then, one evening, Heather complained to me that she was "A little cramping" in her stomach .I then rubbed her stomach until she fell asleep. The next morning, I was awakening to Heather's cry for help! I ran down stairs to find her BLEEDING while using the bathroom, I immediately called **911**…Heather was also complaining of "Dizziness". I tried to comfort Heather as best I could. But she was losing a lot of Blood, and I felt helpless. Then the ambulance arrived, and Heather was rushed to the hospital. When Heather arrived at the hospital, the doctors treated her and controlled her bleeding. Unfortunately, Heather had suffered a Miscarriage…

I was just happy that Heather survived! Sadly, after her miscarriage we did not attempt to have any more children. I never blamed God for this event, but we were fortunate that Heather recovered from this tragic event. We were thankful to God for the "Gift" we did have, our Christina.   And, that was good enough for us!

After this scare, we would continue to enjoy each day in our lives…And have fun too!… We would go to movies from time to time. I especially love a good comedy. I would embarrass Heather and Christina in my reactions to the funny scenes in the movie. I had this Loud Laugh that would linger for awhile after the scene was over…Needless to say, Heather and Christina would want to move to another section of the theater away from where I was sitting! Since I was driving, they had to stay until the end of the movie!

We would try to do as much as we could together as a family. The restaurant was taking a lot of my time with the demanding long hours that was needed there. (*Which I would later regret missing some of the family gatherings*)

As Christina was continuing her education, she was also growing up with the same looks as her Beautiful Mother! This in turn, was getting the attention of the 'Local Boys" around the neighborhood. This made me start practicing my Pistol Shooting skills… (*Just kidding, I already knew how to shoot…LOL*)

What we were most proud of was how Christina was pretty popular at school. Christina was involved in Swimming, and also won numerous competitions while playing the Clarinet in the School Band. Heather would attend Christina's competitions, which made me feel like an idiot for not making the time to also attend. I was so proud of my 'Little Girl." I wanted to make it up to Christina on her upcoming Birthday…

On her **16th Birthday**, I purchased my Daughter a "Special gift". Christina received…A New **2003** Ford Mustang Convertible …The look on her face was Priceless! You see, in my family (*growing-up*) we were not able to get all the things we wanted as children. I wanted to give my

daughter everything (yes, *spoil her*) that she
wanted…And, why not? I had a successful
business at the time …And, I had no wants for
myself!

I tried to make sure my wife and daughter were
taken care of. I remember Heathers' Brother stated
"he respects me, because of how well I have taken
care of his sister". I was happy to hear that
coming from him…Because, he was like
"CONGRESS" in the Family!

And so, for the next few years, Heather and I
continued to work hard trying to keep up with the
daily grind of balancing work and home. Overall,
with a little "BUMPS" in our Marriage *(we all
have them, No marriage is 'PERFECT"),*

I was happy in this Marriage. Just as the priest
asked us when we took our wedding vowels "for
better or worse" So far, GOD has provided for me
with a pretty good life. A wife, a healthy
Daughter, and a Nice home in the suburbs just like
my aunt and uncle have in Pittsburg. And, a
Family Business to add to our Blessings…
More than I could of imagined growing up in the
tough area of Detroit!
What more could a man ask for? Life cannot be

any easier right?

Well, what entered next in my life? I did not ask
GOD for…
But, GOD was not to play a role in this…It seems
The *"DEVIL"* had something for me also
(By the way, how is your "Glass of Wine?"?)

Chapter 9 (Enter…"THE WHORE"…)

It was Thursday, **OCTOBER 30, 2003**
"DEVIL'S NIGHT" (*no kidding people, it was
on this date!*)My wife and daughter were planning
a trip to see one of my Daughter's friend's in
BOSTON…I could not attend because of our
business.

That day they left to Boston for the weekend.
I, after the business was shut down for the
evening, did not want to go home to an empty
house. So, I arranged to go out with some buddies
for a few cocktails. (**FYI**… "Night's Out" (*with
the Guy's or Girl's, without your Partner, is as
Dangerous to a relationship as going down the
highway in …the wrong direction!*)

Some of my buddies agreed to meet. I arrived at
a local tavern to have some drinks. After we were
there for about an hour, some of my single friends
were hooking-up with some ladies at the bar.
Then, this woman walked up to the bar.
I overheard her say to the barkeeper "Do you have
a towel" (*she seemed to have spilled a drink on
herself*) I look over at her, and she said "Hi"

I respond with a pleasant "Hello"… and these words that I will never forget! She said; *"what is it, that when you get married, the sex stops?"* I was Floored! I was thinking "what kind of question is that for a woman to say to a strange man" I was looking around in "Amazement" …

I responded "are you talking to me" (*yes, just like De niro in Taxi driver*) she replied with a smirk; "YES" and had this Seductive Smile on her face…I then replied; "you must be married?" She shook her head "yes"….I added; "And, YOU ARE not having enough sex with your husband?"…She replied "Yes"…and gave me this look that you would see on soap operas when a woman looks interested in you….

She was "Drop Dead Sexy" Dark brown bedroom eyes, Huge Breasts, Nice Figure, and Petite…Maybe **4`6"**…Those words about being married and not having a enough sex rang true to me also…You see, over the last few years I was "sleeping on the couch" …Not because I was in the "Doghouse" with my wife, but in the last **8** years Sex in my marriage was like maybe "**5** times a year!" Mainly because Heather and I were either too busy or too tired from the long days at work…So, Sex in our marriage was "LACKING"

I then started a conversation with this woman. Just flirting *(I was known to 'flirt a lot')* I asked "what is your name" she replied; "**TINA**' I answered "my name is Scott!"… Then as the conversation continued, I noticed that the conversation with this woman was more geared to the conversation of"Sex"…However, I thought I have everything under control, that this is not going to lead anywhere…Right?

We are just "Flirting" As the conversation continues, I mention to this woman that I "Owned a local carryout Italian Restaurant in the area…She noticed that I was at the Bar with a "Celebrity friend" from a local sports network here in town. Needless to say, she was Impressed with my "Status" in the area…*So, here is where my conversation with this woman gets to a 'Dangerous Place" and my morals go straight down*!

I start talking about the subject that this woman is more interested in talking about…SEX! And, let me tell you, the conversation becomes …well, X-rated! This woman wanted to "Feel" how LARGE I was…Then; I start to get entangled in the web this woman was creating…

I start reasoning with my actions…my wife and daughter are out of town, I wanted to see where this conversation goes with this woman…. Tina continues to tell me about her desires in the BEDROOM, and I give her some of the Details of my bedroom manners *(Alcohol is not to blame here! But, it does contribute…)*

So, here I go again…*"Mr. in control"* I lean over towards this woman…And, "she starts kissing me" I was surprised! Then in an instant, we start making out in the Bar! I know what you are thinking, but, this is how it happens…first you flirt, and then…stupidity creeps up on you!   That was a stupid move. I then ask her; "What are your friends over there going to think about us kissing? Tina replies: "They won't says anything I am going to Chicago with that girlfriend next weekend for a ladies weekend".

Then she added; "And, if she says something to my husband…well, she will not be going with me". So, after a few more "making-out minutes" Tina said; 'My friends say they are leaving, so, I got to go.   But, here is my cell phone number, call me when I get back"…I was in a state of

"SHOCK" about the chain of events that just unfolded ...

I then thought, is she for real? And, is she really married? And if so, where was her HUSBAND? I knew my wife and daughter were out of town. And, I am thinking; what the Hell am I doing with this woman? I cautiously take her number. I then proceeded to put her number into my phone. I knew not to put her number into my pocket! I then threw away the paper with the cell number on it...Tina proceeded to leave with the friends she came with...

After this "shocking event" I walk out of the bar to go home (*my buddies already left me*) As I look across the parking lot, I noticed this "Tina" yelling at her friends saying; "I am going with him" Then, in a "fast sprint" Tina runs over to my Car...I open the door for her to see what is going on...

Tina jumps into my Car! *(meanwhile her friends come over to my car, and tell Tina that they are going to call her husband and explain that she left with "some guy")*

She replied; "go ahead" he won't care! I was shocked to see her behave this way.   I found

Tina's action to be a little unmarried like! I found it hard to conceive that her husband would let his "WIFE" just go out to a bar with the prospect of her maybe "Hooking -up" with someone. Needless to say, I was a little confused.

*This is where my life really goes to crap....*I ask her "So, Tina, where do you want to go?" She said something like "anywhere" (*I honestly do not remember, this was happening too fast!)* So I ask her; 'Do you want to go somewhere for us to be alone? She replied: "yes" and added; "let's stop and get something to drink" ...

So I am thinking 'THERE IS SOMETHING WRONG WITH THIS SITUATION?" I am now intrigued to find out where this is going! I stop at a local 7-11 and buy some Drinks. Then I drive her to a.... local Hotel *(yes, I know what you are thinking about me now...and I would love to tell you I was ...ahh Drunk, or...She forced me...)*

No, I was thinking how far This "Married Woman" would go with me...So; I ask Tina...'Do you really want to go through with this?" She replied; 'Yes, why? Are you scared?" Well, I will tell you this, no man wants to be asked by a woman if they are 'Scared" about the thought of having Sex…ESPECIALLY, After all my macho talk back at the bar about my bedroom manners! I answered; "are you kidding, I will make you organism **3** to **4** times!" Tina replied; "I am looking forward to it!"

After I removed my *penis* from the position of a "Low jack" from the steering wheel, I went inside to get a room for the evening!   While I am giving the information to the clerk at the Hotel, I get these feelings of both guilt, and excitement! I was feeling guilty for the Sin I was about to commit in my marriage. I was also feeling the excitement of having possible Sex with this woman I met tonight!

Here again, I start to rationalize with my behavior; "My wife is not going to Catch me, and, nobody will tell her". So, here goes nothing!   I get the room card, and I go out to get Tina. She gets out of the car, and smiles all the way to the room!

After we entered the room, Tina goes to the bathroom to "Freshen up". It is here that I look at myself in the mirror and say to myself; "What the fuck"…Is this "Really" happening? Tina finally comes out of the bathroom. We now begin the process of taking off our clothes.

Let me tell you how this process of taking our clothes off went. First, we both removed our own clothing. No, we did not rush into each other's arms and embrace like we are finally together. No, we just both slipped into bed, turned to each other, kissed, and then had a **2** hour Sex Marathon!

And, that was it! She was willing to go longer, but she realized that it was about 2:30 am in the morning, and she had to be home soon (*And my 'pacemaker" needed recharging*)

But, I will tell you, I have not had sex like that in a Long Time! *(This is how all the getting to know you sex is)*

We both put on our clothes and left to go back to the car. I was at a loss for conversation with Tina. I was thinking this to myself, I went from a friendly Hello, to "all the way to SEX" ...yes, this 'married woman" had sex with me. And yes I, this "married man" had sex with her also... felt Horrible! I had committed a HUGE SIN..."Adultery" and I was feeling really ashamed of myself

(*After the event I felt ashamed, No one feels guilty*

until "AFTER "the Event)…I felt that I had Broken my Marriage Vows to the Lord, and to my Wife!

Now I have to look at Heather knowing that I am a Cheater! I was ashamed…But, just when I was starting to feel even guiltier, something said to me "well, you do not have to tell her". I then thought well "This will only be a onetime thing, it's not like it is going to happen again"…
I bet you are thinking…hhmmmmm maybe this is not going to be a "One time thing" (You might want to add some Wine to that glass now)….

I asked Tina "can we keep this a secret?" she replied; "of course, you think I want my husband to know". I then asked Tina "where do you want me to drop you off?" Are you <u>ready for this answer?</u> She replied; "Drop me off at the end of my driveway"…I was…. Baffled!

I said; "where is your husband?"(*Thinking he is out of town)*…Tina replied; "<u>At Home with the kids!</u> I thought "what?" …her husband is at home with the kids? "What the fuck Kind of WOMAN is this?" I thought to myself; "What kind of husband would let his wife just go out on a Thursday night, and does not give a crap if she comes home at a decent hour?…I just found it hard to believe… I thought; "this woman must be on the verge of Divorce" *(if, she isn't already)* because this did not make sense to me…

So with that, I drop Tina off **AT HER HOME WHERE HER HUSBAND IS WATCHING THE KIDS?** as she asked…When we arrived at her Home, I noticed that no one turned on the lights at the home, or looked out the window to see who is dropping her off!

Now, I just figured her husband is either "Stupid" or *does not Care… (That will be answered at the end of this story). And trust me…her husband WILL BE the "SMART ONE" in this Story!*

Chapter 10 (Disease starts to 'spread")

The next day arrives…My wife and daughter return home after their trip. Everything proceeds as normal. I was slowly forgetting what I have done behind my wife's back.

About **10** days later, I get a call from this Tina. We start another conversation, and after this conversation we plan to meet again. I was thinking…after all, this must be a "man thing" I also thought this must be one of the "Perks" for being successful, I see it all the time on Television… I thought I got away with it already after our first meeting. And the Sex was great! So, we plan on meeting again. The next meeting is AT MY RESTAURANT! *(Yes, another stupid move you're thinking)…*

Tina came in while we were closed between **2 pm** and **4 pm**… (*We were to use this time to restock the restaurant) I had sent my daytime person home at 1:30pm so I can prepare the Restaurant 'FLOOR" for Tina)…*

Hey, if you thought in this story I was going to paint myself as an "Innocent Person" well, I was a person thinking I could take advantage of the situation!

At the restaurant we have more Sex! As we are putting our clothes on, Tina and I start a conversation about each other and our families. Tina told me that her Husband worked as an Architect. And, that she was a Stay at home mother…She also stated that she use to be a Secretary before she was told by her husband to just stay home and take care of their kids…

Later, I witnessed her "Secretary Skills" first hand. After watching her skills as a 'Secretary", I came to the conclusion that she must have been doing *"something other than the normal"* secretarial work for the company she worked for. Because, she did not even know how to "Turn on a computer' less enough use one!

As far as a stay at home Mom…I would also later witness, that she could/would not cook a meal (*she would rely on Carry-outs and Microwave food for the Family!*) I also noticed later, that she was never cared about what her kids were doing on a daily basis!

She also added the information that she was "Given an allowance" by her husband.   But, he was "Cheap" and he was "Boring" …So I thought, in a nutshell is that her reasoning to want out of her 18 year Marriage?

She also added some Disturbing information about her Mother and Father. Tina stated that her mother and father are Divorced, and, that her Brother was going through a Divorce, and she added… that her Brother "Cheated" on his wife too! Soooooo….I am now "Getting the Picture" No one in this Family is "COMMITED" in their Marriages…

I then asked Tina about our first meeting, and how in the world we ended up sleeping together. She replied; "well, my marriage with my husband is over anyway". I asked her why she would think that. She continues on to say her husband was "more into "BIKING" than having SEX with her".

I thought for a second, and did not feel she was telling the entire truth about her Marriage (*I will soon find that out later*) I was thinking that this woman is trying to paint herself as a "Good Wife" just being neglected….

Here she is screwing me, and who knows who else. Because the way she came up to me so bluntly, there may be others too! I continued questioning her…

I asked Tina about her recent trip to Chicago…She replied; "my girlfriend and I danced, and made-out with a few guys". With that statement folks, let's me further know that she is a cheating spouse, that is just looking for a sex partner on the side! Problem was I thought this woman was 'Beautiful. She was also Cute, and she had a Great Personality… I was really into the Sex with this woman…

FEELING that I had gotten away with meeting this woman for sex, I set-up another date with this woman. Only this time, on a week night when I would normally go out with the guys to the Local Racetrack…

Therefore, we start a *Sexual affair*. Sex was the main course during the time we would spend together…We would have sex in bathrooms, hallways, it did not matter. I felt like I was getting away with it. I felt my wife was not suspecting a thing!

Then one evening, Heather came into the restaurant unannounced. Tina had just left, and my wife looked around to see if anything looked out of place. And behold, .She…"found a used condom in the trash"…I was nervous. Heather became so angry that she was shaking"…Heather then asked; "What is that" I thought real quick and replied; "I had someone here that gave me a hand job" (*a Stripper hired by me for one of my buddies*)…

She asked why I had her give me a 'Hand Job" I stated; "Well, I did not know that that was going to happen" I added; 'But, I used a Condom" (*like this was going to be to some assurance*)… Heather then looked at me, shook her head, and asked me if I had sexual Intercourse or kissed this woman. I replied "No". And for some odd reason, she forgave me. Maybe I had Bill Clinton to thank (*No joking, but this was a serious blow to our marriage*)…

And now, I was now getting careless with Tina. After this event, I was getting the feeling that Heather is now aware of me doing some "Unmarried -like things". And, that she would be watching me a little more closely from now on ….

I informed Tina that we have to stop meeting at my Restaurant. As I continue this affair with

Tina…We now meet…at her home! Yes, while her husband was at work. I would go over to her home and we would have Sex! The main thing we would do together is "have sex". Having sex with this woman was becoming a habit…But, some of the 'Sex Toys" that Tina had been…Well, "Unusual" Tina had a variety of sexual devices that made me wonder if she was a Sex Addict!

She had *Ropes*, *Whips*, and a little device Called a "Busy Bee". I asked Tina about this device, and what it is used for. Tina stated that it was a "Vibrator"…I thought for a second, and asked this stupid question; "is it for infants that are horny" She laughed and replied; 'No silly, it is for a woman" I then thought if this was giving her pleasure, then 'size does Not matter!"

I put this **2 inch** vibrator back in its case, and had more sex with her…Now, I was not thinking about anything but having sex with this woman!

But, after I had seen all the Sex Gadgets that Tina had, I was wondering if this woman was a potential "Health Threat"… So, now this is worrying me…I also start thinking,

I have to end this affair with this woman before

my wife finds out!

I ask Tina to meet me at my Restaurant. When she arrived, I said "I think we better call it QUITS". Tina replied; why, "I am in love with you"...I was like...ah..."No you're not!"....She then stated; "I was at the local bowling alley with my Husband. And, I could not stop thinking about you"...To my amazement I was shocked, but flattered! She then said; "I am the best thing that ever happened to you" and "if you break it off with me, then, you are not meant to be happy"... (*Remember this sentence folks!*)

I thought "Wow"...that really had me thinking...is this woman my "Soul Mate?" Did I make a mistake with Heather? I know we had a lot of fun together (Sex) but is this woman for real? Or, did my common sense leave my body like a condom?

Here is where I think I needed my Father's "SLY-RAP" Because I was about to enter a phase in my life I never thought I would...

I then said..."Well Tina, What do we do next"?...She reveals her plan of us being together...She said that soon she would tell her husband she wants a divorce, then she will wait for me…Well, I start thinking to myself "she will be waiting a long time, because, I did not plan to ask my wife for a "DIVORCE" any time soon…

Because…Well, I did not feel that this woman was good enough to replace Heather! So, with my Common Sense absent…we continue seeing each other…When we would call each other we would always call Private Call on the Cell phone so our Spouse's would not know who was calling. (*Remember this trick, because a "Private Call" will be used again later in this story*)

Now we are seeing each other more regularly. And we are going to places where I would introduce Tina to some of my friends who also thought she was cute, and had an outgoing personality, something that Heather had "Lacked"…Tina and I could go into a room full of strangers and make friends real quick because of our outgoing personalities. As we both get accustomed to seeing each other, I start getting even sloppier with the affair.

We start calling each other with *regular phone calls*, and start going out to dinner together around town. And while we were out, some of the wait staff at the restaurants would comment that we looked like a cute couple. Tina would then reply "See, I told you we were meant to be together" I was still not totally convinced about this relationship. I felt that this was not a smart decision because I was known in the area, <u>married, and with a family!</u> And was the <u>Owner of a popular restaurant in the area.</u>

By the way...do you need more wine?

Chapter 11 (The plot thickens)

It is **January "04"...** Tina (prior to us meeting) had scheduled to go away with her husband and kids for a family trip for a week...Tina says to me; "I do not want to go on this trip with him. I cannot be away from you for a week".

Tina tells me that she is going to tell her husband that she does not want to go on this 'Family Trip". And, she will advise her husband to go with the kids without her, or, they can all go on a later date
(*Which would not happen either*)....

I thought that would be up to her...But, it also sounded Very selfish on her part.   I thought, did her kids' feelings matter in her decision not to go?

So the next morning, Tina called me and landed "A Bombshell"...She said; "Last night, I told my husband that I do not love him anymore, and that we should get a divorce!" I was Numb! I was thinking; "wait a minute that was not suppose to happen".   So I asked her; "what did he say?"...she replied; "He said that he would like to keep the family together with the things the way they are for the Children"… I was thinking she must have agreed to that. But she said; "I told him that it would be best if we divorced. And, that he should move out of the house. And, they would talk soon with the children and inform them that they are getting a divorce!"

I felt like an Elephant just sat on my chest! I could not breathe or answer that comment! I'm thinking, this woman is breaking-up her family of **18** years for what? And, what about her "Free Ride" that her husband has just offered her, as to let things stay as they are.

I then asked her; "what now?" Tina said: "Well, He is moving out and into his grandmother's home to live in the basement in two weeks"…I was baffled…This series of events now has me thinking;

"Why would this man just leave his Children and his Beautiful **4000** square foot house in the suburbs?

(His income was all they lived on by the way…)
And go live in his "Grandmother's Basement?"… Why? Why not as a Man, would you not go and find out who your wife is seeing? Why, why?

(*Again, you will find out later in this story*)...

Now, I am thinking; "this is going way to fast, and now this woman is throwing away her 18 years of marriage" and is ruining the children's home life, just for...SEX?

I thought Tina and I was only having sex, not getting married....Yes, we are seeing a lot of each other. But, I was not at the point to ask my wife for a "Divorce"....why ask him now for the divorce?

Two weeks later, her husband leaves the home to "Grandmothers House"... Tina is now pressuring me to tell Heather that I want a Divorce! Well, I am now thinking; "that was not going to happen"....I did not want to lose my family!...I just "enjoyed the sex" with Tina, that was it!...Besides, I was not convinced that Tina was a woman that could be trusted!...I am also thinking..."If her husband chose to move out of that marriage so quickly...What does he know?" Why would he not "fight for her"...I thought Tina seemed to be the Perfect Woman for any man...She was Cute, sexy, and had a great personality. But, why does her husband just Step aside and not confront the man having a "fling" with his wife?

Well, this tells me that this woman needs to prove to me that she IS this 'Better Woman" in my life. Frankly, I did not think she could! *(Now is the time to add some "sobering water" to your Wine glass)*

While Tina arranges things within her family, Tina asked for me to meet her Mother, Stepfather, and Brother, for them to meet the man that she is really "In love with" I thought this to be a joke. But, I agreed to meet them anyway.

That night of the meeting, I met her Mother, Step Father, along with her Brother. While meeting her family, her mother seemed really concerned about Tina's decision on leaving her husband. Her mother stated that "Yes, Tina's husband was kind of boring. But, he was a Good Father". She went on to say that this was not a good Decision (*Divorce*) for either of us. Tina's mother's "Main" concern was the "effect it (*Divorce)* will have on the children". Tina was consistent about our relationship, and would have no reservations in her words to them that "Scott and I were meant to be together" After we left the meeting with her family, and based on how adamant Tina was with her parents that we should both be together, I felt that Tina must really love me, OR she was a great Actress!

Tina would praise me at the meeting with her family…Saying that it "WAS FATE" that brought us together. As I stated earlier, Tina did not care what they thought about it! And, frankly, I felt Flattered! But now, I felt the pressure…

Now what do I do? I could not bring her around my family, they would think I am Nuts!…All I wanted in my life God has already given me, A Loving Wife, a Beautiful Daughter, A Business of our own, Now, the question is after our "Affair" was I was ready to THROW IT ALL AWAY!

So my Stupidity got even worse….I Talked to Tina about how important my relationship is with my daughter Christina. Tina and I thought it would be a "Good Idea" to tell my daughter about our affair and relationship that Tina and I were having!

I have a WARNING before anyone attempts this: This "DECISION" along with the other 'BAD DECISIONS" I have made already…I will regret until the day that I Die!

I thought this would help ease the pain for my daughter Christina when I tell her mother that our marriage is over! Big Mistake!!!!!!

We all meet for lunch, And my daughter *(being the grown-up here with "common sense")* tried her best to put on a smile, as she pretends to understand what is going on with Tina and I. And Christina kept quiet…. after this event… My next "Dumb Move" was to arrange both of our kids to meet… Yes, Tina wanted to have us all meet for lunch!

After the lunch with Tina's kids, my daughter gave me a look like are you Fucking kidding me? I felt sick to my stomach…Sick to the point that I started feeling lightheaded!…The look my daughter gave me was a look of disappointment…Now instead of easing the pain of a possible divorce, I felt like a "RAT" in the face of Christina for what I had just put her through…

The following day Christina and I looked like we drank vodka straight out of the bottle the night before. Our eyes were glassed over, and we were noticeably quiet at the dinner table. My wife asked us "what is up? Why are you two so quiet?"

I looked at my daughter thinking; "Please do not tell your mother" So, Christina just said; "I am tired, I am going to lie down". I was relieved.

But, I was thinking over and over what situation I have put my family in…And I started asking myself; "why am I doing this to my family" What is so special about this new woman in my life? I do remember while we were at lunch with Tina and her children, that Tina had this weird "smirk" on her face. It was like she was getting her way here!

Now I start to take inventory of the situation…First, Tina and I had an affair the first night me met *(while her husband was home with the kids)* Tina then tells her husband of 18 years that she wants a Divorce *(he was the only breadwinner)* and, he leaves his family and home *(like a good boy)* without a fight!

He left his wife and kids of 18 years like he was just paroled from prison! Why? What did he know? I am now trying to make sense of this. And to add to this confusion…her husband agrees to a "Non-contested Divorce!' And, he agrees to "all of Tina's demands" maximum child support, alimony, A whopping **$1,900** a month in total he would pay Tina.

I would later also observe Tina would note the Payments that she would receive from her husband as "pay day" on the calendar! ....and she also got custody of the children. Tina's husband would also help her with any financing she needed to settle in on a new home.

(*After the divorce was final*) I am thinking..."this guy is a saint!"...But, why?

(*And...Again, you will find out soon...just like I did*)

Don't stop drinking your wine!

Chapter 12 (Tina grows Impatient)

Now, Tina starts showing -up unannounced at my restaurant. Tina starts leaving me cards with hand written messages stating that we were "Meant to be together" and "Not to give-up on us". I was starting to feel that this woman seemed so desperate that she might be unstable enough to go to the extreme and tell Heather about our affair!

Tina was feeling so comfortable with our relationship that she would start informing the employees at the Restaurant what to do with their time…Her behavior was so out of control that she even tried to threaten Termination to one of my *Best employees*!

I started getting even more nervous… Tina is now making a public broadcast of our relationship. Tina also starts asking me to go with her to her family and friend's parties. So, I would stupidly attend these events. And NOW, the rumors start around town… it even got to the point to where my daughter's teacher asked her…"I hear your father is engaged to one of the other students' mom" …Now, I am feeling pressured! Tina's uncontrollable behavior, and pressure for me to leave my marriage, and to finally be with her are mounting! After these events, I had some concerns about this path that this relationship is taking.

I meet with Tina…. and I try to explain to her; "I do not think this would be a good time for me to leave my wife(*Christina was also going away to college*) and I did not want to run out of the house. That would leave Heather all alone!" (*I knew I was a prick, but, I was not that "Cold Hearted!"*)

Tina replied; 'But I already asked my husband for a divorce. And, I am tired of being alone"… I then replied; "That was your decision, not mine". Tina replied; "Yes, but it was so we could be together". I said nothing to that remark, and continued working…Then in a huff, she leaves…

She would call me in less than an hour telling me… "Scott, I have something to tell you" I replied; "What Tina?" She responded with a statement no Married man who is having an affair wants to hear…She states; "I have not had my period yet"

Yes, the ultimate **NO, NO** in an affair…

I was now in way over my Head…I
immediately felt helpless with that statement!
Yes, I did on some occasions forget to put another
Condom on. But, I did not think of this scenario
happening! I immediately tell her; "Are you
telling me that you might be pregnant?" Tina
replied; 'I do not know" I responded;   'I want
you to go and get a pregnancy test kit *(from the
drug store nearby)* And, see if the results are
positive". Later that afternoon, Tina stated that the
results of a test kit found that she was negative for
pregnancy…

I was relieved. But now, I am worried that she
is trying to trap me into getting a Divorce. I
contact Tina later that evening and again tell her
that we should stop seeing each other for awhile.
Tina got Angry! She responded. "Scott, you
cannot keep pushing me away. We were meant to
be together.   And, if you stop seeing me, you are
losing the Best thing that ever happened to you"

I responded with this statement; "You say that
you are the 'Best Thing' that ever happened to me
.Right?" Tina Responded; "yes"…I replied;
"Well, How could any man trust you after the way
we met that night?"

I continued; "why did you come up to me that night at the bar, and make the blunt comment about not having enough sex during your marriage to a total stranger? Was it because you heard I owned a popular carryout restaurant in the area?"…Tina replied; "No, you looked vulnerable" …

I thought "Vulnerable?" I was a little taken aback by that statement. Then I replied; "what do you mean vulnerable?" she said "well, lonely"… I shrugged off that comment… (*You will learn that I should have not ignored this statement*) and I continued; I do not think that this relationship is going to work. Mainly because, we met while we were married! And the way you approached me that night at the bar with the comment about YOU not having enough Sex in your marriage. Also, the fact that you slept with me THE FIRST NIGHT that we met! And especially…While you're Husband was at home with the kids waiting for you to come home!

Now explain to me, How do I know you won't cheat on me too?" Tina replied; "I would never do such a thing, because I love you." I then added; "How many other men have you cheated with since you have been married?" Tina Replied; "None"

My response was; "are you fucking kidding me?" Tina then stated; "Well, I was almost sexually involved with one of the hockey dads. But, I just removed my clothes and could not go through with it" I responded; "What made you not go through with the act of cheating on your husband with this guy?" Tina stated; we both thought it was a bad idea, so we did not go through with it"

I responded; are you finished? Tina replied with a simple "Yes" I then said this; "And you want me to believe that bullshit?" She replied; "But it is true, I swear on my kids!" I then looked at her and said; "You swear on your kids that this is true?" She replied; "Yes" I thought to myself, "that she might be telling me the truth. Mainly because, I would think that she would feel terrible if something did happen to her kids if she was lying"... I know I WOULD! ... *Now Stop! Would you believe her statement that she has "NEVER" cheated on her marriage prior to me?* Well, like an Idiot, I did!...and I then "pulled Tina close to me" and replied; "If I leave my marriage for you,

I want you to know that IF you EVER fucking cheat on me, Well honey, I will not be as LAX as your husband was. Because, I will take your throat out with an Ice cream scoop. I will warn you, because of your 'Cheating Past" I will check to see where you are at all times! Because I do not want to look like an idiot leaving my marriage for someone who is a career Cheater!" …

So, here come her tears flowing like a movie director just said to her "ACTION"… Tina then replies; "But, we were meant to be together, Why would I do that"…I responded; "I will not want to throw my **23 YEARS** of marriage away for nothing. So, if you want to date other people to get the "Cheating out of your system" …go ahead! If I leave my wife, I have a feeling that my Divorce will not be "smooth". Tina then stated' "I love you. I do not want anyone else…I want to be with you no matter what" (*remember these statement folks!*) With those promising statements, I was feeling a little more convinced that Tina was telling me the truth. Later in our relationship, Tina would always use that response whenever I would question her loyalty in our Relationship.

Chapter 13 (Heather knows best!)

NOW, it is **FEBUARY '05"** and....all "Hell breaks loose" for me...Now, my ...Nightmare starts.....I arrive home from watching the Super Bowl at a friend's home. Heather is standing waiting for me at the *kitchen sink*. Heather was smoking *a Cigarette*, and it looked like *one of many*! And says; "where were you?" I replied; "I was watching the game at a friend's house" Heather then replied; "Who was the woman that you hugged at the door?" (*She was thinking it was a lover, it was actually "my friend's girlfriend*) I replied; "what were you doing? Spying on me?" Heather replied that she "was following me".

I then asked; Why? She replied; "I have my reasons" Next, Heather goes on to the next question... (*And this is a blow to the gut*) "Whose number is ###-####?"...I was thinking "How in the hell did she find that number'" So, I replied like any Cheater would reply..."where did you find that number from?" she said; "your phone, I looked it up and that number showed up "many times" on your phone". I replied; 'That is my buddy's number"…She then asked…"So, Is your buddy's name "TINA"… I was floored! My heart was beating very fast. And, I was starting to Sweat. What now, I was thinking….

The beautiful woman I promised to GOD to love, honors, and cherish, till Death do us part. The mother of my Beautiful Daughter is asking me who I am talking to (*meanwhile the look on her face is looking at me like I am a piece of garbage!*)

I had no other choice but to *tell her everything!* (*She even pulled-out a bible for me to swear on*)…

I told Heather when and how Tina and I met. And, what led up to everything…After revealing the truth to Heather, we both started to Cry. I cried from Guilt, she cried from Shame. Heather then said; "I want you to call that 'WHORE" and tell her you told me everything, and that it is over!" I said, I will, But, why do you call her a WHORE" …Heather replied,

"Any married woman that sleeps around on her husband, I call a "slut". But, a married woman who cheats on her husband with a married man, especially while her own husband is at home with her children is a "WHORE'. Because she is destroying two families!" Heather continued …"You men think with your dick! A WHORE can "MANIPULATE" you to get "what they want"

That bit of information had me thinking???? If that is true, Then, What does Tina want from me? Then I start to think this…Well, let's see…I have a Successful Business.   And, because of this I got to know a lot of Celebrities in the area. I myself was also treated like a Celebrity in the area because of it. I had Money, Power, and Wealth. Along with a great lifestyle! Hmmmm?

Now all this is making sense to me…I was like…WOW, I never thought about that…I then thought to myself; "Now I got it!…Tina was looking for a relationship with someone that had everything that she did not have in her life…MONEY, POWER, and WEALTH.   And, I was Exciting not boring… (*This is what Tina said about her Ex-husband, that he was "Boring" and "Cheap!"*)

I remember what Tina said in response to the question…"Why did she come-up to me that evening"…Her response was…I was "VULNURABLE!" Which I now felt was not

"Lonely" but, a Sucker!

With that "awakening" I went to the phone, dialed Tina's number, and told her; "I talked to my wife, and told her everything…

And, it is over!"…Tina started to cry… Tina stated "how can you do this to me, my kids are now involved, how dare you do this to us"…I replied; "I feel you brought the kids into this relationship because you wanted to show them a "Bullshit" reason for your divorce!"…

Tina responded with a "Hang-up of the phone call" I was relieved! But, I was also sad. I did not mean to hurt anyone by my act of stupidity. But, I wanted to save my marriage and the relationship with my family. I did not want to hurt Tina, or any woman for that matter… But, I knew that I made a bad decision to have an affair.

Now, I thought it was best to end it, and, save my Marriage. Heather then looked down to the floor, walked over to me, looked up at me and "KISSED ME" and said; "we will get through this, I am going to bed" Heather then drank a glass of water, and went upstairs to bed.

Now, I am feeling Relieved…I just dodged a "Bullet"…I was caught in an affair, But, I was able to fully explain it to my wife. And, Heather was willing to forgive me. I was now thinking to me; "That was not so bad, Heather forgave me for being an IDIOT!"...

Now, we can work on making our marriage work after this incident....Well, not so fast, this forgiving woman must not have been sleeping the whole night after this "traumatic experience"... Heather had the whole night to think about what 'really can get us through this.

Or, if *she ever really could forgive me*, or forget what I have done in our Marriage!

So the next morning, Heather started hammering me with questions about the affair...Heather was constantly asking me over and over about "THE WHORE". And, "how could you do this to us"...She was right! I remember feeling like Crap every time Heather would ask me the same questions Over and Over again ...I was on the defensive every time she would ask me those questions...

We agreed to go to a Local Marriage Counselor. And explain our situation, and try to work out this experience with them...

Meanwhile, it was a few days since I talked to

Tina. And ironically, I was feeling lonely! Yes,
can you believe this? I am now finding myself
'Missing Tina"…. I missed the words such as; "I
love you, we were meant to be together, all of it.
*(Because now, I was beginning to feel like a
"CRIMINAL" in my own Home because of the
affair)*
I called Tina and said; "How are you doing?"
Tina replied; "How do you think I feel, you said
you loved me"…I said; "I do not know what I
want. All I know is I got to see you"…So, yes, I
am again deceiving Heather! I am going to see
Tina. All the while, forgetting about what my
wife had said to me*(for us to work through the
affair)* All the reasons to stay and work on this
marriage are now going out the window because I
am missing Tina!…You are now probably
thinking *"YOU PIECE OF SHIT! You told Tina
that it is over! Your Wonderful Wife Heather
forgave you. And now, you are betraying her trust
again! All great statements…*
But, I was again as Heather stated; " …thinking
with my DICK!" And, I knew with Tina, Sex was
going to be on a daily basis. And I liked being told
that I was loved. I did not want to miss out on the

woman who claimed that she was the "best thing that happened to me"!

So, I continued with the affair with Tina. A few days later, Heather (*not knowing I am back with Tina*) suggested that I go see our Priest. I acted like I was still interested in forgiveness. I agreed to see him the following Monday.

On that Monday, I went to visit our priest from our local church. When I arrived, I proceed to tell the priest that I love my wife. But, I explained to him that I am now having feelings for this other woman. Our Priest thought for a second, and stated the following to me; "Scott, the feeling you have for the other woman is only LUST not LOVE…

He also stated: "How do you think Eve got Adam to eat the apple that Adam knew could be bad for him? I knew what he meant. But his words were falling on "Deaf Ears"

After hearing his familiar analogy (*from bible study*), I replied to him "your right father, I will do the right thing…thank you!" As I left, with my tail between my legs…I knew the words our priest was explaining to me was true…

But after this meeting with our priest, I

continued making plans to see Tina that evening a "friend" was having a birthday party… He was a **D.J.** "friend" (*more about this guy …later in the story*) you see, I did not pay attention to what was really happening to me, and to my Marriage!

Later that evening, Heather calls me in a panic! She stated; "Scott, I know that you are going to meet that "WHORE" this evening, and I want you to come home now!" I thought, "How in the Hell did she know this?" I was puzzled! I tell Heather that "I am just meeting some friends". Heather said; "If you do not come home right now, do not bother coming home tonight!" Then Heather 'hung up the phone!

I ignored Heather's warning and went to the party with Tina. That evening I did not go to my home. I stayed away for two days to let things "die down" Or, in other words 'Let Heather cool down" …But, when I did return to my home, Heather was "SILENT"… not a word was mention to me about that Thursday night. Heather and I do not talk for two days!

Chapter 14 (Divorce Papers)

March 08, 2005 I go to work…And, I am thinking what Heather is up to? WELL, Heather's next move was "Divorce papers" served to me at my business. Now, the realization of losing my Marriage is here…It is really happening, I am losing my Marriage, and I start to now wonder what is ahead for me. I contact a lawyer about the Divorce Papers that I have just been served. My lawyer told me to continue to stay at the home, and avoid any "Confrontations" with Heather.

I took his advice, and continued to stay at the home. And I will tell you, it was very "uncomfortable" sharing a home with a spouse that has just filed for divorce from you. And, I am sure it was "uncomfortable" for Heather.

Here she is just finding out that her Husband of **23** years is seeing someone else…She MUST want me out of her sight **ASAP**! Even my dog Kippy did not run up to me when I came home… Now, she would only come to me if I had Food!

Chapter 15
(NOW, as my Nightmare continues)

(This is where you stop drinking and pay attention!)

The date is **Monday March 21**[st] …I arrived home at about **3:30pm** in the afternoon. As I am pulling-up the driveway of our home, I notice Heather's car in the garage (*you see she normally works until **6:30 pm***) As I enter the home, I notice Heather leaning on the kitchen counter with a "weird" look on her face…I asked her "what are you doing home?' She replied; "I left work early" I replied; "is there anything wrong?" Heather just shrugged her shoulders…

I proceeded to get some extra clothes (*you see, I have not been home the last couple days*) I was shacking-up with Tina…

As I walked over to Heather to have a conversation with her, she then asked; "How is your "WHORE" doing?" I responded in anger. And, an argument started. As, the conversation became heated, I asked Heather; "why are you getting me angry?

I then looked behind Heather, and noticed Heather's purse had a "Portable Tape Recorder" sticking out of it... I asked; "what the hell is that for?" she said; "that is for work, anyway, the recorder is not on" I knew Heather's Job did NOT involve tape recordings... I was eager to see if she was telling me the truth. I then reached for the purse, Heather yelled for me to get back, and pushed me away from her purse, she grabbed the home phone. She then proceeded to called **"911"** and claimed I was becoming "violent", and that "They should send over some officers"

I am thinking this is not a good thing, so I felt it was time to leave because this was not the HEATHER I KNEW acting in this manner...I then grabbed my clothes and left...Later that evening, a couple of officers came to our Restaurant to question me about what happen at the home.

After the officers questioned me, they advised me "Not to return home that evening" I did exactly as they asked, and got a Hotel room for a week. I stayed in a local Hotel room away from my home of 18 years that I was not welcomed in.

On **Friday March 25**[th] just three days since the incident with Heather, I was served with a "Personal Protection Order" **(PPO)** at my Business! I was in Shock! As I read the reason for the **PPO**, I read these allegations of Abuse, Threats of Violence, and...... the Statement that I told my 'Daughter' that I was going to New York TO KILL SOMEONE?   I could not believe what I was reading!

I immediately contact my Lawyer about the Personal Order and its contents, and we schedule a Hearing. That day, would be the last time I was allowed to enter my home of **18** years....

And now, I am in the beginning stages of total loss.... I have been kicked out of my home, and Heather is accusing me of being a "Monster" to boot!   And, Tina is getting her wish...A few weeks later; I was to attend an informal Hearing on the PPO... My Wife and her Sister go on the stand and *well, they were not completely..."Truthful"* ...Stating on the stand that I was a "Threatening and Abusive Husband!" My wife even Staged and took pictures of my Pistol (*I had gotten when I opened my business **10** years prior legally for protection*) in a threatening pose for the Judge…showing my pistol in a place my Daughter even testified was never ever placed there by me (*a food pantry of all places*)!

I was waiting for Heather and her sister to also state that I knew where "Jimmy Hoffa" was buried!

I then got angry in court. Angry because of the way I was being pictured in my marriage. *And frankly folks, I do not recommend getting angry in a court of law!* And, because of my angry tone, the judge then granted the **PPO**, and added these "parting words for me" ….He stated; that I was "my own worst enemy"… (*I guess he meant my looks were enough to scare most people…So, my Lawyer should have asked me to come to court in a Priest uniform!*) and then I thought…Well, I guess if he was going to use how I looked…Then, that is something I could not change or argue!…

After hearing Heather's testimony, I knew things were not going to go as "smoothly as Tina's divorce"… I have now (because of my actions) turned a good woman into a <u>SCORNED WOMAN!</u>

Now that my wife has a Personal Protection Order against me. And, by the court granting this to Heather, I was not allowed to go anywhere near our home, or go near Heather in any Public Place...or to even see my Dog!

I was not to contact Heather in any way shape or form...or any of her family... or our FRIENDS! Because if I did, that would be a violation of the court order! Now, I am out of the home.   All I had was a few articles of clothing and that was it! I was cut out of the family altogether!   Heather was scorned, and she was turning everyone against me. I had no way to defend myself to anyone.   No, I was not trying to defend my INFIDELITY. But, all the accusations about me being a "Threatening and Abusive Husband!" in the **23** years of our Marriage. I never threaten or laid a hand on my wife, daughter, or anybody else in the family for that matter!   But, I was (*by court opinion*) A "Monster"...All of our friends were now only "Heather's friends"...And, no one from Heather's family tried to contact me to see if they could help in some way! Nope, I was "Dead to them"

Now, I have to prepare for the next step of this "Nightmare", and that was Divorce Court! I am now *(because I am "Homeless")* forced to move in with the "Woman that I was meant to be with". As I am living with Tina, she witnessed firsthand what has now happened to me, and states the following; Well, you should of left your wife the same time that I did" I was taken aback by that statement, So I replied; "What do you mean? I added; do you think that my Divorce would have been "EASIER" if I left a year ago? I continued; Tina, I told you my wife will not "Be as gentle" as your husband was in your Divorce" She replied; "Well, he knew it was over" I looked at her for a second, and thought...

I think he did know it was over, *But, not how she thinks!* Because, when her Husband first met me a month after he moved out of the house, He greeted me with...'*A HANDSHAKE and A SMILE*" I thought that to be kind of ODD!

(*More about this later*)

Chapter 16(Tina gets her wish)

Are you finding this exciting yet?

I am now preparing for Divorce Proceedings. This was stressful. The Divorce papers were a lot to deal with. My lawyer and I were gathering documents, going to hearings; frankly it was a mess…

Because of the everyday stress of the Divorce proceedings and I was neglecting the business. The community also heard about what I have done to my marriage. With all of that going on, I was forced to close our restaurant! I now thought, GOD, what have I have done! I then ask GOD for help! But, I think at this point, God was tired of my "STUPIDITY"…He gave me all the Warnings and I Ignored them all! Yes, I was getting "Exactly what I deserved"

While Heather's Lawyer and my Lawyer go back and forth with Papers…I now have to face the prospect of working for someone else for a living…After a few failed attempts to keep steady work, I finally landed a Position with a Local

Mortgage Company. (*Ironic, since I was without a home of "my own"*) Now, my lawyer and I were ready to go to 'Open Court" to have our Divorce heard…Then, a few days before the proceedings Heather's lawyer…….

A little about Heathers lawyer,
Heather had hired a "GREAT (*LIAR*) I mean…"LAWYER"…you see, I believe most Lawyers are 'Professional Liars" They are to blame for the 'WARNING" Labels on everything! Because, if *McDonald's* did not put *Caution this cup of Coffee is* 'HOT" on the top of all coffee lids, than some "Dumb Fuck" will sue them for "Millions" because that person is…well, a "Dumb Fuck!"…So, enough of that bit of info….Back to Heather's Lawyer, He was the "County Prosecutor's Father!" Yes, the same county we were going through the divorce! It was like "Going to a Gun fight with a pocket knife" Well, this (*Liar*) I mean "Lawyer" contacted my lawyer and now wanted to go through an Arbitrator instead of an Open court. Her Lawyer must have known that having our case heard in 'Open Court" That would mean…all the information would be "Documented"… That is… by the Court!   Which

would have put a stop this Smokescreen of
accusations of Abuse and other "Untruthful"
things that I was accused of? (*The ONLY real
crime that I had committed was "Adultery" which
I admitted to in court*)...

Since Heather was the 'Plaintiff' and we had to
abide by her Lawyer's "bag of tricks". Heather's
Lawyer along with his other list of things stated
something strange to my Lawyer. *I should note;
prior to the hearing, the arbitrator who was
presiding over the divorce asked my lawyer "Is
Scott going to bring a* **GUN** *to the proceedings?"*
(*Is that what* **PRE-JUDGED** *means?*) He added
that he had a 'Potential Buyer" for our Closed
Restaurant?
This was confusing to my lawyer and me.
Because the Restaurant was closed **5** days PRIOR
to this Offer...There was NO Restaurant to
purchase in our eyes! While I was working at the
restaurant, I never talked with such a buyer that
was interested. So, who 'Negotiated a sale?"

I had my lawyer investigate who is looking to
purchase our 'Closed Restaurant". When my
lawyer was able to get the "Offer to purchase", I
asked my lawyer; "Who is the Potential Buyer?"

My lawyer informs me of the individual's name. And, behold…it is one of Heather's Relatives! And, that this person was offering **$75,000** to purchase the "Closed" restaurant!!

I was baffled to say the least. Then I asked my lawyer; "Whom did he offer this price to?"…My lawyer responds; 'Heather!'"…

Well people(*in case I might have lost you here*) let me explain what this now means…You see, Heather stated in court papers that she had…. "No Knowledge of the Daily activities of the Restaurant" even though she was the Secretary, also she Prepared and Signed off on All of the tax statements…But, if (*as Heather stated in Court Papers*)she did not have "Any Knowledge" of the Business, Then, how could she negotiate and come up with a selling price for **$75,000?** And for a Closed Business to Boot!

I will explain a little further what the Motive for this is… You see, now that Heather's (*Liar*) I mean 'LAWYER" has a 'Buyer' for the restaurant, which means that the selling price of the Business is now brought into play as an ASSET to split as a "Martial Asset". Now, any 'Simple minded' Judge would see what is going on here, But, *not our Arbitrator…*He must had owed my wife's lawyer a *'Favor'* And, allowed the "Potential" Purchase of the Business as an asset!

Well, folks if this was told to me by anyone else, I would not believe it!   But, it is true! I was getting Gang Banged by the system! There was no Vaseline to lubricate my Adultery Committing Ass! Yes, Heather was going give me the best fucking than any of the one's she ever gave me in our entire Marriage!

Now, we are testifying under oath And, <u>WHEN OUR ARBITRATOR WAS NOT SLEEPING</u> I kept dropping my Pen, in efforts to wake-up the judge. But, He must have known the results BEFORE the Testimony, and was catching up on some much needed SLEEP!   Heather stated in court that I was not only an Abusive, alcoholic, threatening, Murder for hire thug, but I was rarely at Work and that SHE supported the family?

Now, let me set the record straight! I worked an average of Ten Hours a day. With that, I was also suffering from a Hernia the size of an Orange protruding from my Belly Button

(Which in fact, Heather's angry rant caused her to

CANCEL my Health Insurance Policy when she filed for divorce! This meant that I would have to pay for any kind of Surgery Out of pocket for my Pre-existing Condition) There were nights I would lie on the floor at work, and Ice Down my hernia to ease the pain!

In the Eleven Years our business was open (*and, while Heather did not work there?*)we were able to afford all the pleasures of New cars, jewelry, Front Row Concerts, Dinners, Shopping sprees, and Mortgage Payments, Food, on just Heather's **$30,000** a year job? Well, Heather threw in that she received an 'Inheritance' from her Deceased Parents that she had to use to support the Family! She must have forgotten that we used **$20,000** of that Inheritance Money to play in the Stock Market (*which we eventually lost*)....

But, that information was not brought into play in my case! I was in a War that was Un-winnable! As Heather continues her testimony. Again, Heather stated that she had nothing to do with or had any knowledge of the Business! Yet, she was able to "negotiate' a sale price of **$75,000** for the

Business she was not involved in? Heather even denied knowing about the T-Shirts that 'She Created" for the Restaurant!

I just had to sit there and take it like a ...Man? Well, when I testified, I was able to prove that I did not have any Secret Bank Accounts or Hidden Assets! No, I had nothing put aside for myself! I gave "EVERYTHING" to Heather and for our Family! My Lawyer and I had SOoooo much evidence to prove she was lying (*and still have*)...

My Lawyer and I were able to produce Documents to prove that Heather participated in numerous restaurant business transactions...I even had Witnesses there to testify on my behalf... But, even with all this "Evidence"... It did not matter; I was going to lose this case!

And, in the end...the Judge gave Heather *Everything!* Oh, Wait... he gave me my "Closed business" And half of the personal home items (*which I never took or wanted*) and, the judge ordered me to pay half of Heather's credit card debt!!

In addition, the Judge put a LIEN on any monies I received for the Lawyers fees... **$38,000** to be exact!   Yes, that is right! **$38,000** in

Lawyers fees…For what should have been a Simple Divorce!   There was no Spousal or Child Support involved….Just **PPO** Hearings, and Divorce Proceedings, that was it!   I think the total Division of assets was as follows: Heather **+$182,000**, Scott-**$2,000!**

Yes folks, I got "Punished" by the system….And, frankly I deserved It!   But, all I ever really wanted in these proceeding is to clear my name. I did not want any money, or any part of the home! I did not want Heather to win by 'Not being totally truthful"

But, it was all my doing… Yes, I caused her to become angry and dishonest in our divorce… Because of my "Infidelity"

Now let's keep track: I have managed to lose my *Marriage of 23 years*. I lost *my home*, lost the *respect of the community*, my *friends*, and now my *Business of 11 years is gone*. I am by 'The Courts Opinion" a LOSER!

I am getting the feeling that I am no longer in control of my life.

And, now for the "BIGGEST BLOW" in this mess that I created……

I lost *my Daughter's Respect*!   Christina stops

calling me and answering my calls…The reason for this is simple. My Daughter believes that since Heather 'Won" in Court, she was thinking that everything that Heather stated in Court was True! Even our friend Bart pulled my Daughter aside to tell her he did not know how 'Horrible of a person I was"

Now that Christina lives with Heather and Christina was raised within Heather's side of the Family. Since none of Heather's family communicates with me, why should Christina?

I think they all hope that I would "Die Soon!" Well, frankly…Not having my Daughter in my life is basically a 'Death Sentence" for me. I know Heather is happy about that! I created this for myself. I knew that Heather was angry, but I was not prepared for the Goodies that she would throw into this Divorce Case. I do now! I am only thankful that Heather did not ask for the *Death Penalty* because, who knows, she might have gotten that too!

But, even though I committed the act of 'INFIDELITY' in my marriage, and that has its consequences as you have just heard about. (*More 'Surprises" yet to come for me!*) But, 'not being truthful" under Oath' ALSO has its consequences. I hope GOD forgives them…Because, if it wasn't for my 'INFIDELITY' any of these events would have taken place!

<u>By the way</u>…**FYI**…After the court proceedings, the potential buyer backed out on the purchase of the Closed Business….

I was shocked!!! I could have now sold it to him for…A cup of Coffee! What a joke that was…You see, back when the 'Offer" was made, the 'Buyer" could have just dealt with the Landlord of the leased space for a lot less money(**$2,500**)because the Business was "Closed" if the Lying Rat was *really* interested in the first place!

Forest Gump and even *Rain Man* would have realized this was all a 'SET-UP!" I am left with the main reason for this mess that happened to me! I have…The woman I was "*Meant to be with*"…. "TINA"

(Hey, are you learning anything yet? Don't worry, the Real Mess is forthcoming!)

Now is the time to drink some "Whisky" too!

Chapter 17 (Grass Greener?)

For the next year and a half I shacked-up with Tina... As I am now living with her, Tina starts to show me signs of what a "great woman" she is, and why her husband exited <u>Without a Fight!</u>   I have now adjusted to working for someone else (*after years of being self employed*) and now with paying Lawyer fees and back bills along with two car payments! And contributing to my new household....My credit went from great to poor very fast...I had to *Defer Payments* to stay on top of Bills...My headaches are coming more frequently.

To add to my dismay, my daughter one day, decides to 'drop off" her new Mustang that I was making payments on (*her mother thought she would need to establish credit for herself...Yeah right!)*

So, Here I am with two cars to deal with...Well, as if my luck would could not get any worse, I had to turn over the Mustang to the dealer.(*repossession*) And, when I could not pay all the mounting bills from my divorce, I lost my own car to the same.(*Repossession*) Now, I was without a vehicle to get to the odd jobs that I was doing.....Thank goodness for Tina's older son, he allowed me to use his car for a few weeks. (*I eventually rented a Truck from a friend*)

After those setbacks, I start doing regular activities with Tina and her children, (*they were good kids...I believe because of their Father, and other close relatives as I would witness later. They were ALL just more "Victims" from this mess*) ....

While observing Tina with her Children, I notice some Parental Issues with this woman. It seems Tina was not capable of preparing meals for her children. (*I did that, or the kids would grab a "Frozen Dinner"*) Tina was not really concerned about the welfare of her children, as I thought she should. In other words, making sure that the Children had proper supervision.

I also witnessed that Tina would without any hesitation, and without any guilt, leave them Home Alone without concerns for their welfare in case of an emergency! I was not used to this kind of behavior. I knew Heather would put our

daughter's welfare first before we did anything!
What Tina was more concerned with was the
number of times that we would Have Sex.
(*Remember, I still suffered with a HERNIA in the
middle of my stomach that was the "size of a
baseball" that made sex a little painful at times*)
Tina thought it was *just fine.* So, Sex is what got
us together, and, that is what we both wanted
right? Isn't that the reason for my Divorce? Yes,
but, there has got to be more in a "Relationship"
besides Sex? Well, Tina wanted it all the time!
She was so open about us having sex, I was
feeling a little embarrassed around her children.
Tina was into wanting to have Sex at all hours of
the day.

Sometimes she would almost "openly" let the
children know we were going up to the bedroom
for Sex! Tina had a sex drive that was a little
"Disturbing" to say the least… there were nights
that we would have a "Normal" sex night (*for
Tina it was at least one hour*)…then, in the middle
of the night, she would reach over and touch my
"JEWELS" while I was sleeping… (*I felt like I
was next to a "Michael Jackson"*) I really had an
issue with this…

One morning (*after an evening of a "Sex Marathon"*) Tina wanted to fool around before I went to work (*I only had an hour before I was to report to work*), after I explained this to Tina, her response was

"So, you are turning me down again"

I was disturbed by her comments...I thought, what the FUCK is wrong with this woman! She had a drawer full of sex toys so, why this Shit! Tina's Sex drive kind of reminded me of the "man eating plant" in the movie *Little Shop of Horrors*! Only, it was Tina's Vagina yelling; 'Feed me, I'm Hungry!" just like the Man-eating Plant in the movie, Tina was always hungry for more Sex! I had a hard time satisfying her NEEDS! Tina one time suggested that we should have a '*Threesome*" to spike up our sex life. I told her that I was not into that kind of relationship. I mentioned for her to stop that kind of *nonsense*...Well, that statement made me think if she was to cheat on me, she better get with a man that "*Just got out of prison*" so he would have enough" Energy" to *keep up with her*! Then, if I was to hear '*screams*" coming from the bedroom about him wanting to go *back to prison* rather that to have sex with her again…well, she would then be *caught cheating*!…Ha, ha! But, seriously folks…Having sex with Tina was like 'punching a clock" *(with no overtime compensation)* Hey, the reason for the relationship with Tina was Sex, and she was always willing, But, to this degree? Folks, be careful what you wish for, you just might get it…and more than you DO NOT want!

I then thought of the little Device that Tina had once shown me called a 'Busy Bee" And asked Tina; 'why don't you get your Busy Bee…BUSY?" Tina responded *angrily* that she will!…I then thought to myself; "that busy bee seemed *too small* for Tina's Vagina, I think the Real Sex toy for this woman should be a *heavy duty 100 foot auger with extra lasting force*! Because this woman was out if control with her need for sex!

I could not believe what I have now gotten myself into with this woman! I was now worried that she would start cheating again to satisfy her sexual appetite! And, to make me worry even more, Tina was taking a 'Daily Antibiotic" prescribed by her Doctor? I asked her about them, and she stated; "They are for a "Sinus problem"…Oh really, what "Sinus Cavity" is she referring to?

After finding out about her "Daily Vitamin" I was not only wearing Extra Spermicidal Condoms I would also pour peroxide on my "Dinky" just for good measure after having Sex with Tina.

I would notice over the next few weeks, Tina was starting to wear these Skimpy Outfits…that Tina would purchase from the "Teen Section" of the store that made her Breast almost flop out of her shirt! This made me comment that she should dress more "appropriate" (*Even her 16 year old daughter agreed with me*) But, Tina would not listen to any of the sort. I had to leave that Sensitive Subject alone because that would start another argument! …

I would try to continue to satisfy Tina sexually as much as possible. I left my **23** Year Marriage for her… I cannot fail in this relationship, right? That would mean that I would have lost everything for nothing! So, I continue to try and satisfy Tina sexually…

I see some more disturbing things from Tina… I am now getting annoyed with her shopping habits… No, not grocery shopping, But, <u>Mall</u>

<u>Shopping!</u>
I remember one time when we were preparing to go grocery shopping, Her kids asked; "why is there no food in the Fridge" Tina's response was…"I am on a diet"…I was not sure of the meaning of that response. So, I asked Tina; "Did you say you are on a diet?" Tina replied, "YES"…I thought; "What does YOUR DIET have to do with your Kids"

I was embarrassed for her and her Kids…The Children also had this puzzled look on their faces (*which occurred a lot when Tina would make a statement*)

I noticed how much her children Respected her on Mother's Day….The only 'gift" Tina received on that day was a gift from me! Yes, the children showed her on that day how much they "Really" respected her! Tina was furious to say the least. She would always try to throw it in the children's faces whenever she had the chance…

I think the children really 'threw it in her face" that day. I think they knew what kind of mother she 'really was' … I am now starting to wonder EVEN MORE about this woman's character as a mother(*and her selfish manners*) and, again,…her Sex Drive!

Now…Because of my respect level starting to decline for Tina, my sexual desire for this woman is FADING and I am finding myself feeling like the sex that I was having with her was becoming more in the category of WORK instead of pleasure…

It was now weeks and we are not having Sex. I start wondering if she is back to her cheating ways of the past …Remember, when she first approached me that fateful night… she was this "sex deprived wife" I am again questioning myself if I am really with the right woman in my life. My friends continued to warn me to keep an eye on her, because they thought she was up to no good! Especially, since my friends knew I had LOST EVERYTHING in my divorce! And they thought Tina might be bored with our relationship!

With those warnings from my friends, I continued to try and please Tina's sexual appetite! And, to add to this mess…I am missing my daughter Christina! So, here is Tina's take on Christina… Tina stated to me; "Christina only comes around to get money from you"…I

Thought about it, and, thought "No, my daughter loves me" But, If this is true, then, I must find out for myself.

I then, called my Daughter to confront her with what Tina had suggested to me. Christina and I argued. Now my Daughter, who I wanted to see as much as possible, stated that "she has not come to see me because she did not want to come around if I was with Tina".

Because of Tina's great advice, Christina and I do not speak to this day! Now that I do not hear from my little girl, I go through most of these days in complete loneliness.

And (*like clockwork*) when I get in my car and turn on the radio, I hear this song; *"you had a bad day"* playing all the time, while I am with Tina! , I started to see that the "grass was not as green" on the other side. I will add… Tina could not hold a candle to Heather as far as motherhood! Now this person has put a "Stake in my heart" by her analysis of Christina's and my relationship!

Here I am, in a 'Completely new life". I am finding it hard to adjust to…I have a new woman and her children, and, I am having all the sex a

man could ask for!   Because of Tina's Sex drive,
I would have to "Perform" for her even though I
was suffering with my hernia. (*Thank GOD for
"TUMS"*)

    I continued to serve as a "sex slave" for Tina
(*I seldom came to a Climax*) As we continued
with our RELATIONSHIP, Tina would watch
shows such as, The *Bachelor, Real World* (*all
teenager shit*), and if that wasn't enough, Tina
would buy all the *Gossip Magazines* like *People,
US,* and any other of the *Glamour Magazines*
along with one of her favorite shows; *Cheaters*
Hhhmmmmm!   I noticed Tina would Daydream a
lot! She was also talking about plastic surgery and
Botox Treatments!   I started asking myself
WHY? Why would she feel a need to such a
thing? Does she want to look younger to attract
someone else? I would always assure Tina that
she was already attractive. This woman looked a
lot younger than her age (**46**) …

    Why did she feel the need to look younger?   I
asked her; "Tina, do you want to look younger for
some other man?"…Tina replied; "I could never
see myself with another man" she added this
statement of reassurance to me; "I get

"Nauseated" with the thought of another man putting his hand on me" So, with those words, I thought I need not worry.
Because she seemed Believable!

Well, as you will read further,
She will be '**<u>Vomiting a lot</u>**' as anyone would after what she eventually chooses to do!

Now as Tina and I try to live our life together as a "Happy Couple" and eventually get married...Because of all I went through (*Divorce*), even though I was getting TOO MUCH SEX, I wanted to make this relationship work!
Tina and I thought it would be a good idea to visit a Marriage Counselor to help us deal with both of our "Issues"... and, in doing so, help us prepare for a Happy Future together...(*So I thought*)
Tina and I pay a visit to a local *Therapist*.
When Tina starts explaining her reasons for the visit, Tina stated that she was not happy with my recent lack of affection(*I called it lack of "Sex" Tina called it a 'Lack of Love"*) Tina stated to the therapist that she was in a "Different Place" in her life?... Needless to say, I was a little confused

with THAT answer Tina gave to the therapist. When it was my turn, I was asked by the Therapist about my issues. I stated that recently I have not been able to keep up with this woman's Sex Drive. And, I was in a State of pain *(mental)* from my recent divorce, lack of communication with my Daughter, and (*physical*) my Hernia. The therapist stated that if we both wanted this relationship to become stronger, we should allow each other 'Some Space" and this will allow our relationship to maintain a balance…I was pleased with the therapists' suggestions, except for the suggestion of a possible Medication for me! (*I think Tina was hoping that it was for a prescription of "Viagra!"*)

The therapist concluded that because of my recent Divorce I could have some sort of post traumatic Stress Disorder and, suggested that I might want to either increase my exercise or take an Antidepressant…I thought about the two choices, and eventually chose exercise. Tina never explained to me the statement she made to the Therapist of being in a different place in her life?

I would soon find out later, that this statement

meant 'literally"
Chapter 18 (Back to her "cheating ways")

After our sessions with the Therapist, life continued to evolve around Tina. I would try to keep the reason for m*y recent misfortunes'* happy!

I would take a management position at a local Comedy Club/Bar. You see, during my Divorce I needed some 'laughter" in my life, so I took an interest in *Stand-up Comedy.* I participated in some training classes to learn how to be a good *Stand-up Comedian.* After getting to know one of the owners of the local club, he offered me a position there... while working in this establishment, I met some new "Friends" whom frequented the Bar area of the Club. The Bar area was known as *Menopause Manor... (By some of my friends)* the reason for that particular name was because most of the Clientele was over the age of "Forty". And, most of the men that frequented this particular bar were looking for mostly "One night Stands" with the older woman that would come into this place.

This bar was no place for couples that were in a "Healthy Relationship" Why you may ask?

Well, because, there was always someone lurking in that bar that would sleep with you at a moment's notice! Yes folks, I picked a nice place' to work. A place that had all the Sluts and Whores your heart desires…. and Tina and I both knew this, so we knew not to come to this place alone. Why? Well, because of what I stated prior…Because of the *Sluts* and *Whores* that hang around in this place!

When Tina would come to visit me at work, I would always have Tina stay close to our new "Friends" to be safe! They were not the kind of everyday friends in my life, but they were pleasant to talk to from time to time. I did notice most of them were either divorced or in bad relationships.

There was an incident one New Years Eve, when Tina's ex-husband's new girlfriend was there at the Bar with some friends celebrating the New Year. I had a 'Drink" sent to me from Tina's ex-husbands' new girlfriend? The odd thing about this was that I was the only one that was sent a Drink! Tina noticed this, and took the drink that was sent over for me back to her ex-husband's girlfriend. Tina was insulted! I had a feeling that the girlfriend of the ex-husband was trying to tell me something? Tina and I ignored her, and the rest of the night was uneventful.

Most of the time, people would hang around the bar and have conversations with one another.

One in particular stood out, He was a Disc Jockey from a local **FM** station. He would hang out with these new friends that Tina and I met. He had this kind of "perverted" look about him. Now, I am not claiming he IS a "Pervert", I am just saying he would *Fit the look of one...you know the look, wondering eyes, that when he looked at you, your skin would "crawl" (He "Definitely" had a face for Radio)* HE was *Overweight* and sported this *Scruffy Beard*. What really stood out about his looks was that he wore this weird looking "Hairpiece on his head". It looked kind of weird *(like a "sloppy haircut")* But, All the patrons liked him because of his statue in the area (**DJ**)...

Tina and I thought he was a nice guy to talk to, and would have conversations with him from time to time.

I remember one evening, A Woman that he was seeing at the time, became angry at him. She was

"Lunging" toward him. I thought that she was going to beat the crap out of him. I pulled her off of him…I thought that she might try to embarrass him and "Pull that thing off of his head" But all that was avoided…

I never got the scoop from him about what her problem was with him that night. While I continued to work at the Comedy Club/Bar, Tina would show-up and go over and chat with the **DJ** and the others while I was working. I mean these are 'My Friends right?" so, I thought, 'what would be the harm right?   Well, before I go any further with this story, I want to tell you a little "History" about a couple of these "Friends"…

One evening, I was returning from a Comedy Gig. I stopped off at a Denny's Restaurant for a Quick Bite to eat.   It was about **2:30 am** in the morning, and I was starving! I find a seat at the counter. And while placing an order of food, I notice this "DJ" and another "Friend" named Jerry.

A little history lesson about Jerry, real quick; "He was in a *on again /off again* relationship with his girlfriend named Lisa. One day while Jerry and his girlfriend were on the outs, Lisa called me at my restaurant to apologize about Jerry's "Bad" behavior the prior evening. Jerry had a "Big Mouth" and I was willing to help 'Shut it for him" I would later learn that Jerry took her phone call to me that morning as if I was trying to "take his girl" from him! Well, with all due respect, she was not my "SIZE" if you know what I mean....But; Jerry would always try to make this an issue with Tina and me, which would sometimes put a strain on our relationship! So, enough about Jerry...

Now, as I say "Hello" to the **DJ** and Jerry while at Denny's, they introduce me to a 'Friend" that was also present with them. She was a 'Miss Michigan" Runner-up of a few years ago. Yes, and she "Looked just like a pageant contestant!' "Gorgeous" They were at the restaurant having a bit to eat (*or so I thought that was the plan*)...As I continued to enjoy my meal, all of a sudden, I hear Jerry throwing insults to this beauty queen! And, she starts to cry...

I thought, what is going on? I learn from the group that this *Miss Michigan* is married and met these *Two Jokers* at the comedy club/bar that I worked at. They invited her out for a bite to eat and to "Talk" about her suspicions that her husband might be seeing a younger mistress and possibly cheating on her…

Now I start to "Get the picture!" After talking with this woman, my suspicions were correct! It seems that these two (*the **DJ** and Jerry*) were trying to coax her into partying through the night with them! They were not trying to "Quiet her fears" (about her husband's possible cheating ways) they were fueling her suspicions to lure her to sleep with them!

With this information, I asked her to come over and sit next to me. After she moved over to where I was sitting, the **DJ** and Jerry walked out!(*they must have figured that I was too good looking of a man for their ugly mugs to even think about competing with me for a chance with "Miss Michigan!" That is, if I was looking to cheat!*)

I feel they assumed that she was going to come home with me! But, that was not the case! I was IN A RELATIONSHIP. I knew the all too familiar effects of cheating and I was not going to cheat on anyone, anymore! Especially, cheat on the woman that was "meant for me" …Tina! *Miss Michigan* and I talk a little further, she would go on to tell me how these two 'Friends" invited her over to the **DJ**'s place to continue 'Talking"… I then recommended that she "talk to her husband about her concerns, and maybe the two of them should seek some counseling" I told her 'Not to cheat" on her husband, if she really loved him. And, she should find out the "Truth" first, and hopefully, things will work out for them! *Yes, I am now a 'Marriage Counselor" and, I think after what I have been through (Ugly Divorce)* I figured, Why not… *Miss Michigan* thanked me for our conversation, and gave me "a hug". After I finished my meal, I asked the woman if she would like me to 'Walk her to her Car?" She replied; "yes, thank you" So, I did just that…And, that IS ALL that Happened that night!

We did not "exchange phone numbers" or make plans to go and have some "fling' either!

When I returned to Tina's place right after this event I explained everything that happened! Tina was concerned that I was not telling the truth and maybe I cheated with this Miss Michigan. I asked Tina to call Denny's, and talk to the Waitress that served me and the group. I stated that the waitress witnessed everything…But, Tina did not want to discuss it any further and we went to bed.

Tina would bring this event up from time to time but it would eventually be a *Non Issue*. Or was it?

Now, back to my story… one evening after visiting our "Friends" at the Bar, Tina would ask me questions about the **DJ**.   And, added; how could he ever 'Find Somebody' for a Relationship (*Because Tina thought he had a "Nice Personality" but "Hard on the Eyes"*)…

I replied; "Well, he makes good money. *(He also worked at a local casino for some good money)*And, that might be enough to entice a woman to 'compromise herself" If she was into "Just money".

After this conversation, I am getting concerned about her interest in the **DJ** because, first of all, after hearing what his plans were for the Miss Michigan (*whom was 'Married"*) I did not trust him! Secondly, he did have money, (*But, not looks)* that I *once had* when I met Tina…But, now I am an average Joe with my limited salary.

I thought I was just PARANOID, and dropped the thought…Because, She told me she "left a marriage where she had Money" to be with me, and would live with me in a empty box because 'we were meant to be together"

But later, I would notice whenever we were having some domestic issues; Tina would go to that group of friends (*including the **DJ***) and talk to them… (*A Waitress friend of mine who had overheard Tina making some "Un-Girlfriend like" statements about our relationship to these Group of 'Friends")* Tina's issues; I was CHEATING behind her back…I thought to myself…Wait a minute, I am working at a Comedy Club…And sure, women who would attend the shows would come up to me and say HI… But, Tina was always there at the shows with me. Why the accusations?

When I confronted her with these accusations, I informed Tina that I did not do anything wrong. I ask her why is it that she all of a sudden is now accusing me of cheating. *(Come to find out later, this is how a cheater who "is cheating" acts when they are the actual "CHEATER" in the relationship!)*.

In the weeks to follow….I find Tina looking for things to show her displeasure in our relationship. One day, I stopped by a local florist to bring Tina some flowers

(*No, I did not do anything wrong!*)

When I arrived at the florist, I saw the most amazing "Yellow Roses" that I thought were beautiful. So, I bought them! But, when I gave these beautiful roses to Tina, She replied; 'So, we are 'Friends' now?" I was taken aback by this statement?

So, I asked her; "what do you mean?" Tina replied;

"YELLOW ROSES MEAN "FRIENDSHIP"...I explained to Tina that I did not know this when I purchased them, but she was angry! She took this as a sign of disrespect to our relationship! I felt that I was trying to do something nice for this woman, and now wish I had bought the latest edition of playboy and a six pack, and jerked off instead of doing something nice for this unappreciative *Bitch!*...

After this failed attempt to keep our relationship happy, I now start seeing Tina hanging around a troubled female co-worker (*age 30, Tina was 46*) and, Tina starts changing her schedule at work, sometimes starting an hour earlier, sometimes later. Tina started taking a Weight loss over the counter pill to help her lose some unwanted belly fat she was getting over her tight jeans...I explained to her to just stop wearing her undersized pants that would push out her belly, and that she would be fine. She was no *Spring Chicken*, nor was she **20** years old, so wearing those size pants made her look fat!...But, she was not hearing anything I had to say, and continued to take her weight loss pills. And continued wearing her *Abercrombie* jeans...

Sometimes, Tina would go out to a MOVIE THEATER on a Friday night *ALONE*, which I thought that was *ODD*...What person must see a movie that bad to go alone? I would go to a chick flick with her if she wanted to see one...I have gone before! But, I knew that if I question her about it, she would make the statement that I was being too jealous! So, I did not mention anything of my suspicions to Tina.

Tina's place of employment was having a "Company Party" that Tina was to attend "Alone" with some other Co-workers...That night after the event, Tina came home late, drunk, and, her hair was out of place. I asked her how the event was. I then noticed that Tina had a Woman's ONE SHOE in her hand! I asked Tina; "How did you end up with a woman's one shoe?" Her response; "well, one of the girls left it at the baseball game" I then asked; what made her leave in so much of in a hurry that she left her one shoe" Tina replied; "her boyfriend picked her up at the game"

I knew this was BULLSHIT! Just as you are thinking; I thought; how did this woman walk out of the ballpark" without knowing she had only one shoe on and, how did her boyfriend know "the location of the section in the ballpark where she was at"...Tina's story was not believable.   I wanted her to continue and explain this nonsense to me... But, I realized I needed to stop this conversation right now. The main reason...Tina was drunk and was not making any sense. So, I just dropped the subject...And, went to bed!

Over the next week, I would find some of Tina's "Sexy Underwear" on the floor near the bed(*knowing very well that she did not wear them to bed with me on those nights*) and, those panties had the look of "Being torn" in the area of the crotch!   Tina's answer to the panties on the floor was "the dog" got them out of the dirty clothes ...

But, I know that Tina would put the dirty clothes

in a basket that was "**18** inches high" …That would mean the dog used a well planned attack (*with a coat hanger*) to get to her dirty panties! So I thought …
"Hey that is a 'Very talented Dog" she has! "
That same dog must have left those "*New Cum Stains*" on the sheets too!
Again what a very talented Dog!

Tina's Cell Phone would ring "in the middle of the Night" that would make her JUMP up so fast…like she was awaken from a nightmare. But, I should not be concerned…it must have been some *Silly Willy* dialing the wrong number again…But, it has been occurring around the same time, **1:45am** for the last two weeks…

Again, I am just being a *Silly Willy*… NOW Folks, what do you think? Should I be worried that all my suspicions about her CHEATING again are now true?
But, I was now a 'Patient Man" willing to let this LYING BITCH hang her own *NECK!* And, if she was cheating, what will my reaction be?

Chapter 19 (The "Private Call")

You might want to add a 'Prozac' to your drink for this shit!

The date is Monday **September 24ᵗʰ, 2007** and that afternoon I spoke with Tina (*She would always call me at least **8-10** times every day and after ALL conversations say "I love you"*) I arrive home from work at about **8:00 pm** and ask Tina to "get dressed, and let's go out" (*To celebrate the big Commission Check I have just earned from work*)

And, as fate would have it...Tina receives a "Private Call" on her cell phone. When I saw the incoming call on her cell phone, I asked Tina; "Who could be calling you on a 'private call?" Tina makes no attempt to answer it (*even though her phone is "ringing" in her hand!*) I continue; "why don't you answer it" she replied "it is my work calling me to change my schedule"

I then thought to myself... (*I do not remember Tina being a Psychic!*) Next, the call goes into Voice mail...So I then say "if this is true, let me hear the message that your "Work" left you" Tina replied "No, I do not have to answer to you"...I was in SHOCK with her response! I replied; "what do you mean? We are in a relationship" Tina replied; "No, You do not control me, we are not married" I asked for her to explain why she is so defensive, and she is speechless...she starts to babble bullshit to me!

I am now seeing the REAL Tina exposed! She had just revealed herself like the mask coming off of Cat woman...and, I am getting angry. Angry because I ignored all the warning signs that this woman who stated to me 'we were meant to be together" is now telling me after this 'Private Call" that she is not going to answer to me?

So, I grabbed all of my belongings that I could, and left the home, I could not let her think that I am an idiot anymore! Later that evening, I called Tina to get an explanation of what just happened...She says;
"I am not in love with you anymore"......
(*This is the silence that followed*.....)

I thought, Wait a minute, when did this 'I do not love you anymore" come into our conversations? Tina just told me Hours before the

infamous "Private Phone Call" that she loved
me…Now; she 'No longer loves me? I was
confused to say the least! I reply; wait a minute,
where do we go from you getting a 'Private call"
to 'you are not in love with me?' No response
from Tina…Hhmmm?

I then ask; 'Are you seeing someone else?"
She replies with this insult of a remark; "No, I am
leaving you, because of you"….I thought for a
second, and replied; "What does that mean? And,
No I left you!"…She then replied;
"WHATEVER"….And hung up!

I never really received an explanation. But, I did
not need one! I knew for sure she was busted
because of the "Private call". She had no defense
except to LIE. Now the picture about this woman
is becoming all too familiar… I knew now that
she had to be seeing someone else *(because of her
Sex drive)*…..Yes, but whom?
*So, are you feeling sorry for me yet? If you do feel
sorry for me…Well, then you are not getting the
message here! I DESERVE THIS…And, there is
MORE to come!*

The next day, I get a room at a local hotel. I

am still in shock of the recent events that transpired just a few nights ago with Tina… Remember her statements of 'We were meant to be together!" After losing my **23** year Marriage for this woman, I could not believe what has now transpired in my life! Now, I start drinking alcohol (*I know this is not good, but I had to try and relax somehow I thought!)*As I stay a few days at this Hotel with no communication with Tina (*which was unusual to say the least, Tina would call me 8 to 10 times a day before the 'Private Call"*)

Later that weekend, I called Tina and asked her to meet me for some coffee, so we can discuss what is going on…she replied; I will call you later. I then wait until about **11 pm** in the evening on that "Friday Night'…with no call from her. I then call her cell phone, and it goes into VOICEMAIL and I continue to call her until she answered… (*I know this is not normal, But, I had a feeling that she was up to no good!)*

Then, the phone is answered, and to my surprise, I hear Tina laughing and she hangs up the phone….I called back and the voicemail states; "Mailbox is full"…Now I am even more angry, because now the alcohol was starting to fuel my anger. I then do a 'Alec Baldwin" on Tina's children's cell phone leaving 'Unpleasant" messages about their mother.....*(I know this was wrong, But, all I just wanted was for someone to tell me where Tina was!)*

I leave the hotel room to find Tina ...And, hopefully SEE this person that she is now involved with! As I was looking around some of the local places, I thought...*Hey, go back, and leave her alone.* Besides, I was too drunk to use any common sense anyway!

The next morning, Tina called me!...And, I asked her where she was...She replied; "I was out with some friends" you know them, and we went to a comedy club"....*(That would explain her laughing)* But then I asked; 'Which friends were they" She replied; 'All of our friends from the bar" I asked if she was there with 'a date" She replied; "NO' I was just out to "have some fun'....

So, with that I just "hung-up" I had a hard time believing that she was there without a date! So, we were 'taking a break' I thought...you know... Some space! Well, a week or so later, one of my close friends and her boyfriend spotted Tina at one of the restaurants that we would frequent at the mall…and, Tina was there with another Man!…

I was (*needless to say*) angry! I then asked this friend, "What did this guy look like" She replied; He was *Fat, Ugly,* and had a *Weird haircut* she continued, "You know, the haircut that had the "just got out of bed look" I then asked; "how old do you think he was" My friend replied; "**50** something" …

I am felling a little too familiar with the description of this *New Guy* in her life. I wanted to call Tina to get the scoop about what I just heard…But, before I could call Tina, she called me first! I hold back telling Tina about what I just learned. While Tina and I were completing our 'How are you doing" call…She ASKED; "Have you heard anything from your 'close friend?" My response was; "Yes, she said she saw you at the mall with some *Fat, Ugly Guy* with a *Bad Haircut*"…She replied angrily, "Don't believe a word from that bitch!"…I replied; "Well, that bitch that you are referring to has "no reason to lie"…And, you have shown that you are "A born liar" Because every time you open your mouth, 'LIES" COME ROLLING OFF YOUR

TONGUE!

I continued; "You have been seen by many people around town with some 'Fat ass with a *Dead Animal* on his head" She replied; "Well, me and this *New Guy* are just friends" I then asked her who he was, and she stated this: "He is a divorced, **37** year old man that one of her girlfriends introduced her to" I then asked; "where did you meet him?" Tina replied; 'you are going to laugh when I tell you"

I was puzzled? I then asked; 'No I won't laugh, now tell me where you met this *New Guy*? Tina states: At the "Comedy Club BAR AREA!" I was enraged, I replied; "You mean to tell me that you met this *New Guy* at 'Menopause Manor?" Tina laughs and states; "Yes, I met him on 'Sweetest Day".... (*That was only "2 weeks" since the 'Private Call incident!*) I was speechless to say the least! Tina had this kind of excitement in her voice, as if she was telling one of her friends about some "Great News" about this new man in her life!

I could not believe what was happening in my life! Most of all, I start Remembering: ALL THE BULLSHIT this woman had said to me throughout our relationship…Were meant to be together, and 'our love is forever', How she stated that "I get nauseated if another man touched me" and the infamous… "I can never see myself with another Man" … Bullshit!

I cannot explain the 'Rage' that I was feeling at this time! I was so angry that I could….Well, 'PUT MYSELF IN A CORNER" for time out! Because, I was not going to Jail for this RETARDED WHORE So, I (*after a deep breath*) replied; are you sleeping with this '*New Guy*?" She replied: "NO" which was bullshit! I knew that was not the case… Remember: the *Torn Panties* that I found, and the *movie trips alone,* the s*chedule changes* at work, things started to add up! Then, I asked her this *Final question*: "So Tina, is this the end of us?" She replied; "well, remember the saying; If you love someone, let them go, and if they come back, it is true love" I thought for a second, and in my head came up with a better analogy to this situation…..This woman is a 'WHORE" and let her go….and, if she tries to come back….get a restraining order on her!

Now is the time that I start putting things into

perspective….I am getting EVERYTHING that I deserve! I cheated on my wife, and the woman I cheated with is now… <u>"Cheating on me!</u> Ha, ha shame on me! Like the old saying "once a cheat" *Always a Cheat!"*

So, here I am… Let's do an "Inventory" of what I lost…my marriage, my friends, my business, my respect in the community, my daughter, and for what? A WHORE…Now she is back to her 'cheating ways"…I NOW start to pray to God for help. I ask God to help me "Fix things"…and I hear and see NOTHING! I can only hear my tears hitting the floor! I look at myself in the mirror and want to throw-up. This is the nightmare that I created. What do I do now?

I look back at what got me here: it was the words; <u>"what is it about being married that your spouse feels it is not important to have sex with you anymore?"</u> Yes, "THE WHORE" led me to my destruction, just like Sampson and Delilah, I was a fool to think she was the one for me in my life…and now she is moving on, Moving on to another <u>"vulnerable person"</u>…I am now ashamed of myself at this point, I try calling the WHORE for one last explanation of why?

She invites me over to her home, when I arrive at her place, I ask her this question......"How did this happen? I thought we were meant to be together?" She replied AGAIN with this analogy; "Well, like I told you before, it was not because of another man, it was because of you" Well folks, to explain what she "*Really Means*" in this statement... AFTER LOSING EVERYTHING (My Business, Money, My Popularity in the area) in my 'DIVORCE", I am now NO LONGER the man that she envisioned as providing her what SHE wanted!... I was now "CHEAP and BORING!"

Remember, Earlier in this story I talked about how Heather (now my ex-wife) did not date me because of my "Rich Status" in life. NO, Heather loved me for who I was, not what I had! And, I replied; "How can you continue to make that statement? I already hear people tell me that you have been seen around town with this "*New Guy*'. You have seen taking him to places that we used to frequent. And, from what I hear from those people, they say that your are either NUTS because of your choice of this *New Guy* (*Fat, Ugly, and with a 'Hairpiece*) or you are trying to

get this guy hurt because you know as well as I do, that if I see you with this guy, I will not just "Slap his wrists"
*(I will call Tina's New Guy a COWARD!
I call him that because of these two
reasons…One, because of the way he contacted
her on that Monday night "Private
Call"…Secondly, Because, this person was
invading our relationship, no matter what was
going on between us)*

I asked; So, what is up?…She then starts with these remarks that would *"Blow up a Lie Detector"*…she says; "I told you…He is just a "FRIEND"…he is **37***(10 years younger than her)* and I only see him 2 times a week" and, we have not had sex yet!…Well, AGAIN, I did not know if this woman just got amnesia, or did she think that she was talking to an idiot.   But, I knew this WHORE'S sex drive (*it would make a "VIBRATOR' run and hide!)*

I then asked her "Remember when you told me you get 'Nauseated" even thinking about being with another guy"…She just looked at me and shrugged her shoulders…Her response was as *Cold as Ice*! She did not care about what I lost to be with her, she knew that she had to get rid of me! Tina knew I was capable of finding out who she was cheating with! And, I would eventually find out ALL the cheating she had been doing (*prior to me finding out on the 'Private Call Day*). Tina realized I would eventually leave her!

At that moment, I could not stand to look at this PIG any longer…I was getting angry and annoyed with her **BS**.

Then, she made a remark that made me want to squeeze the life out of this 'WHORE"…She said: 'why don't you just go back with your wife, because you don't need to deal with my baggage anymore"….

When she made this comment, I was seeing myself "stamping license plates"… I was thinking…what a piece of SHIT! This **Pig** was showing me how much of a *Heartless Bitch* she really is… after all the "*Heartache*" I just put my poor wife and family through. For **This Bitch** to even suggest that I go back and ask Heather to "take me back" was a comment coming from a person that is *not even human!*…To play with people's lives like that? Like it is all a game to her! That was like me trying to "unscramble a scrambled egg!"…

So, (*I knew for my own good*) I had to leave the presence of this person of **EVIL**….with her *COLDHEARTED* suggestion! So, I left her…And with the strength of GOD…"In one piece" I left to come to grips with the situation I CHOSE to put myself in…I got EXACTLY what I should get for cheating on my Wife! I got fooled…. Fooled by a WHORE… And now, I have no respect for myself anymore!

I am thinking "what should I do now?" Do I continue to try and get more lying reasons from Tina's on her decision to move on to some other Victim… or maybe, track down this *New Guy,* with the knowledge of knowing when I did find him, I was going to do some INHUMANE THINGS imaginable to him?

Yes, I was thinking that would satisfy me and I would show him there is no way that this *New Guy* was going to get away with taking away from me the woman that was supposed to be worth losing EVERYTHING for!   But, I had to think of the repercussions in doing this…Because; I was

NOT thinking rational anymore.

So, now I am turning my anger towards the MAIN VILLAIN that was to blame for all this HELL that ruined my life……

I am now planning the *UNTHINKABLE*…

I am planning to **<u>KILL MYSELF</u>**….

CHAPTER 20 (A "Reason to live")

I am thinking of ways to end my "suffering." I am NOW planning to end this NIGHTMARE I have chosen for myself! So, on **November 17ᵗʰ, at 9:30 pm**…I sat in my car. And, with a "handful of pills" I am planning to swallow them and *HOPED* I would die in my sleep peacefully. Or, I could *Wrap a Belt* around my neck and *Hang Myself* in my car seat!

OK now, which one am I going to choose? Now, would be a great time to have "Clarence" (*It's a Wonderful Life's Angel*) show-up and tell me it was *"all a NIGHTMARE"* and, go back home to my Wife and Kids"…No, he was not coming….
I did not even find a red pair (size **10.5**) of "RUBY SLIPPERS", for me to click and say "There is no place like Home"! No, just this lost lonely Fool in the front seat of a Car ready to leave this NIGHTMARE of a life! ….

And, by the way, I didn't hear God speaking to me, telling me, don't do it Scott!   No, not a sound from the man upstairs…. Just me! And, as I thought about the choice of which way to go out of this world, I knew I could not do it! So, why did I change my mind, you ask? Well, it was what "*I did not hear from GOD*" that made me change my mind. God wasn't saying anything.

I knew He wasn't going to answer a person that is turning into a *Coward* and running away from his troubles by killing Himself…I learned at an early age that God does not like *Cowards* (*nor did my Father*). All my life, I "never ran from anything". *(Except when my mother chased me with a belt. or, if I got my Father upset)*I knew I could not end this life that GOD was so generous to give me…I knew I just had to continue on somehow, and wanted to think of a way to rise from the ashes of this HELL….

As I started the car, I turned on the radio. A Song came on the air that I thought was *'Hitting at my current state of mind'* I took it as a Message from GOD.

The song is Called HERO, by Mariah Carey….it was coming across to me so *CLEAR*…this is what

I heard:

> *Oh....Lord knows, dreams are hard to follow.*
> *But don't let anyone, tear them away.*
> *Just hold on, there will be tomorrow.*
> *In time, you'll find the way.*
> *And then a hero comes along,*
> *with the strength to carry on,*
> *and you cast your fears aside,*
> *and you know you can survive.*
> *So, when you feel like hope is gone,*
> *look inside you and be strong,*
> *and you'll finally see the truth,*
> *that a hero lies in you,*
> *that a hero lies in ... you!*

After hearing these inspiring words, I stopped crying. And, I sat straight-up in my seat, and said THIS to God; "I messed up my life. What should I do to make-up for the mess I have created?".....Let's see...I was lost for answers. I did not know anything to think of. For the next few days I was looking for a way to make things right with God.

Then, I finally got one! The following week, after

watching a movie, I got this idea…What if I write a story about the bad choice I made in my Marriage? A book about how I lost everything by cheating!

And call the Book…

BEWARE OF THE WHORE

THAT'S IT! And maybe, just maybe….
I can warn or help change someone's mind if they
are planning OR if they are
already….UNFAITHFUL in their Relationship!
Almost immediately I felt this "warm sensation" comes over me.   This will be my way to *WARN* others, to not make the same <u>BAD DECISION</u> <u>that I did!</u>
But…Before I start anything, I had a little <u>"UNFINISHED BUSINESS"</u> with the WHORE. I had to be sure that Tina really is a WHORE or was it me reading the situation all wrong?

Remember, Tina stated that she left me because of me (*what that means in my eyes was still not clear…*)

Have I really lost the woman that was meant for me?
In other words;
Is she really a "good woman?"

If she is a Good Woman ...she would not do something *Consistent in a Whores Behavior* and..."*Cheat on her new beau*"... right? Well, you will soon find out! I had a plan to see if Tina could be FAITHFUL to her new "FRIEND"

... Here's what I did...

Chapter 21
(Conclusion…the **WHORE** Exposed)

Now it is time for you to get a "Cold Glass of Water" and "WAKE-UP"

I remembered that Tina was taking a trip out of state with her children during *Thanksgiving*. She had a car that was not so good in cold weather. I had *(prior to us breaking-up)* promised to loan her my four **(4)** wheel jeep truck to use for this trip.

In early November, I called Tina. I asked her if she would still need the truck for her trip. She replied, No…at first. Then, she called back and said; 'yes, I would like to use your truck for the trip, thank you". With that, on a Wednesday night, we met and switch vehicles.

When we first meet *Face to face* after all this crap, Tina played a song on a CD for me while we are in my car. The song is named WHO KNEW *(by the artist PINK)*…The song is about two people who meet and fall in love. Then, after three years they split-up, even though *one* promised their love was forever!

I listened to the entire song, and she replied;
"that is like our story"
My first thought was that this woman is living in a
Fantasy world of make believe…then, I grabbed a
CD of my own and played a song called *"Over
You"* by the artist *Daughtry* (*which is more like
our relationship*) she did not respond!
I then said; enough of the *"Head Games Lady"*
and left the car. We then switched vehicles.

When Tina returned to Michigan the following
Monday, she called and asked for us to meet that
evening to switch back our vehicles. When we
met to switch cars, we talked for about an hour
and discussed our ending relationship. She then
stated that we could possibly date again…I was
polite and said "we will see". But, in the back of
my mind, I was thinking; if this bitch tries to
come back to me, *"I WILL leave the State!"*…She
then replied; <u>"Because, there must have been
some reason that I fell in love with you"</u>

Can you believe that comment coming out of
her mouth? This woman that would always say to
me "we were meant to be together" Now did not
remember why she fell in love with me?

Well, I replied…*Hum*…So; I told her I was

leaving. Tina then had the nerve to ask for *a kiss*!...I pulled away and said; *no*, I will take a "rain check"...she then tries to kiss me on the cheek, I turned away and said; "I got to go"...and so she agreed, and we went our separate ways!

My REVENGE is still to come........ Before I start my revenge against Tina, I stopped by a local Gas Station to fuel up. After I filled up my gas tank, I went inside to pay the cashier. When I finished paying for the gas, I noticed the **DJ** in line paying for some stuff. He had some Candy Bars in his hand, which made me think this guy is on a *"Slim Slow Diet"* ...So he says; "Scott, how are you?" I replied; 'Good. "But, Tina and I are over, that *Bitch* was cheating on me"...He replied; "Sorry to hear that, But, have a "GREAT HOLIDAY!"

I had to catch myself for a second...He sounded like he was *Happy* to hear my comments about Tina and me not seeing each other anymore! But, I was in a hurry and I did not want to waste anymore time talking to *"Sweating to the Oldies"*... so, I let his comment go!

Now, it is two days later, on a Wednesday night. I receive a phone call from Tina. (*One thing to* note: *Wednesday's are her night without the children*) She then left a message asking me to return her eyeglasses to her home. Tina sounded sick. So, I called her back. Tina stated that she was not feeling good. I then asked her if she would like me to bring something for her. Like aspirin, or soup….She said "ADVIL"…

I stopped at the drugstore and bought her some ADVIL…then went to her home. As I was pulling into her street, I noticed her EX-HUSBAND pulling-out of the driveway…So, I waited for him to leave…I went up to the house and knocked on the door. Tina answered, and I entered her home.

Now my REVENGE is right on course! I give her the ADVIL. I then asked Tina; 'are you sure you do not want me to go and get you some soup or something"…She replied; "well, I would like some *Egg Drop Soup* from the local Chinese restaurant" I stated that I would pick some up for her…But, she said this; 'I want to go with you"…I thought that was kind of strange… I asked why?

Well, it seems she has been watching too much of the *"SOPRANO'S'* and thought I might *Poison her Soup*…I guess she must of thought that

…maybe because of her recent cheating? But, that was not on my mind at all…

We go together and buy her some soup. We then returned to her home… I am now thinking; This is going smoothly….I sit down, (*we do not bring -up Anything about CHEATING while I am at her home that evening)* I then ask; 'What, I do not even get offered a glass of wine for bringing you this stuff'? She replied; "sure, open up a new bottle"…

So I opened one of her favorites *Merlot* …and now I am anxious about how this is going to unfold…..Then I ask how are the children doing? She said "fine"…Then, she asked me… (*Are you ready for this…?)*

"Do you want to watch a movie"…I was shocked! So I replied; yes why not! So, we order a pay per view movie, (*with Kevin Costner*)As we are watching the movie, she is seated on one couch, me on the other…Now I am looking at her and she is "looking from the corner of her eye, to see if I am making a move towards her" No, I am staying put! Now the wheels come in motion…

I then ask her; "do you want a glass of wine"? She replied; "YES" Now I am thinking…perfect!

Now *I KNOW* my plan is *Full steam ahead!*
Toward the end of the movie, and to the bottom of
the bottle of wine, she asked me this; "are you
O-K to drive home, or would you like to sleep on
the couch?" I replied; "Well, I think I would be
over the limit if I drive home" She said;
  "Fine, then I will get some blankets for you".
I then said; 'Where is your boyfriend?"
She replied; "I told you, we are just friends"
I replied; "oh…yeah, that's right…well then, why
don't I sleep in bed with you, I *'Promise'* that I
will not try anything"…She said; "O.K. but, we
are not back together"
  I replied ….Sure, *I know that*…And, to my
amazement we go to her bedroom!   Next, *I am
not kidding you*, as soon as we got into the
bed…"Off her clothes went"…I responded, Wow,
"just like old times"…She said with a smirk;
"Well, this is how I sleep" *(No, this is not how she
sleeps folks…well, not while WE were together)*
  Then I got her in the position where I use to
enter her *'ugly world'* when she stated these
"famous words" that only a "**WHORE**" would
say; "Now, we are not back together" so I replied;
"Yes, I know that" and she continues with…

(*Are you ready for this statement?, because I was not expecting this*)...Tina says; "Because, I do not want you to think I am a "slut" after this"...Well, I am thinking to myself...that is NOT what she is...Then, she asked me this stupid request Tina asked; "*Now, Make love to me*"...I was ready to *Barf* after those words! I thought...What? Make LOVE to HER?

After all that this woman has done to help *Destroy my Life*, She was really asking me to make love to her? After this *Bitch* made this stupid remark, I leaned over and looked closely into her face...While I am looking into her face; I see a *clearer picture* of this woman. In this picture, I see all the lies, and deceit that this woman has in her *resume* called life.

I was shocked that I could not see this clearly before. I now saw a woman who is revealing to me her *True Identity*....And, for the first time in this relationship; the face is that of a **WHORE!** Yes ...I had made a fatal mistake in my life. I now know what her true self is! She was *Exactly* what I WAS AFRAID OF all along....a **WHORE**...*And Johnny...Here she was, Naked* with her legs spread wide open and ready to have

Sex…Not with her new man, *no, no, no*! But, With Me!   ….
(Hey, she has to be consistent in her behavior, Heaven forbid that she was to change her real self) I was now seeing the ugliness that was inside of her showing on the outside.…

I was taking one last look at this "little in statue" woman who was able to give me the worst "Beating of my Life"…Yes, I CHOSE this **WHORE**. But, I felt like she sold me a fake bag of goods! I was thinking of putting a pillow over her face and ridding the earth of this no good piece of garbage.

But, I know that you cannot kill anything that is already dead!

(Evil does not have a Beating Heart)

I was now looking back at all that I lost because of MY CHOICE to have a CHEATING Sexual Relationship with this **WHORE!** Lost, Is More Wedding Anniversaries, the Family gatherings, all my Friends…   But most of all…I lost the most important things in my life…My Wife and my Daughter! Yes folks; she is EXACTLY what my wife said she was all along…. **A WHORE**… So, here she lies…in the only position she is comfortable in…Naked and wanting SEX… the only thing she was 'good at'

And, as I lean over to her,
I Said;

"Tina… She replied; "yes"…
Remember a few minutes ago, when you asked me not to think of you a SLUT'…

She replied; "yes" "And I told that you that in no way do I *think* of you as A SLUT"

She replied; "Yes"…I then said;

"No Tina, YOU are not a **SLUT**…all you REALLY ARE IS…. A **WHORE!**"

I then got off her work area (bed)…grabbed my clothes, and started walking out of this situation of "Pure Hell".

And as I turned away, she threw a People Magazine at me and yelled:
"FUCK YOU"…

I thought for a second, turned around, and replied:

'No, not me anymore'…As I went downstairs, and left her home. I left with the ANSWER to my suspicion…What suspicion?   That evening….I witnessed firsthand, even in her New Relationship she could not be FAITHFUL to her man…
(*This also proved she most likely was NEVER faithful in our relationship*)So, that night, I got my question answered.

Yes, my REVENGE was complete!

I Finally SAW Tina's **<u>TRUE IDENTITY</u>**

Because, that night…

I UNMASKED… **"THE WHORE"**

By the way…

Remember the <u>Ex-Husband </u>of
THE **WHORE**…

(That "ever so gently" left the home without a fuss) Well, as it turned out, he began dating a "co-worker" soon after his divorce. Then, a year or so later, HE married the woman. My educated guess is that he must of known about his wife (*THE* **WHORE**) and was growing tired of her cheating ways (*while they were married*) and hoped that some "Sucker" (*me in this case*)would fall prey to his **WHORE.** And eventually, remove her from his life! Because, HE did not want to be the Villain in the breaking up the Family…So, with the "Handshake" that he gave me when he first learned of my dating his EX (*like I just did him a Favor*)…He just left the **WHORE** ever so gently.   Not ANGRY, but with a SMILE on his face. He just (*without a fight*) chose to move aside and watch everything unfold….

Guess he will be buying a copy of this book too!

As for the Identity of THE **WHORE'S** *"NEW FRIEND"*

Well, I ran into one of the women that worked at

the club that Tina and I would frequent. And, she informed me that Tina and the**..... DJ** are DATING!

I was (*needless to say*)......... Not very happy!

Because having learned this means not only have I been betrayed by the *Whore*, but also by a so called "Friend" of mine...The **DJ!**

Now it all added up for me...The times Tina wanted to talk with this particular group of "Friends" at the bar (*I am sure she fed them the same bullshit WHORES feed most people, just to justify their motives*). The meeting with the new guy at "Menopause Manor", and ...The description of this *Mystery Man* that Tina was seen around town with... *Fat, ugly, and with a Weird Hairdo!* Which best described the **DJ**.

By the way... Tina was 'A little off' concerning the age of her new guy. The **DJ** was not **37**, but more like **50** something! (*Oh well, this should answer the question if Tina was a Good Secretary!*)

Well... as far as the actions of the **DJ**, he

probably was angry at me because he and his friend were not able to take advantage of Miss Michigan that one night. Because of my interfering with the situation...he set his sights on TINA. And, he probably feed into her concerns about me being unfaithful in our relationship.

So, she took it *'BAIT, LINE, AND SINKER!"*

Because, as the Definition states:
"WHORE" Definition: ...an offensive term for somebody who is regarded as willing to set aside principles or personal integrity in order to obtain something, usually for selfish motives.

Because of the **DJ**'s money, and celebrity status...Tina was planning her next move! Because I know if this **DJ** was really a Taco Bell employee (*with his looks*) Tina would not even accept his *PHONE NUMBER*...

Tina is what one of her ex-friend's had stated to me about her...Tina is also an "OPPORTUNIST" and does not care whose life she destroys, even if it's her own kids, to get what she wants!

Now, with the identity of Tina's Real Guy, I

wonder back to the earlier comments that Tina would say to me while we were together(to quiet my fears of her leaving me for another man) Which were; "I get Nauseated even thinking about another man putting his hands on me". **WOW!** She must be throwing up a lot these days after having sex with that *Thing!* My only hope now is that she upgrades the potency of her antibiotics to **1000 mg!**

But, all in all, who cares who she ends up with? I feel what the **DJ** thought he *TOOK* from me, is really what I feel is more of the reality of what he **REMOVED** From me!

Because Tina's Actions spoke *LOUDER THAN HER WORDS!*...And, if I thought Tina WAS a good woman, and he tried to take advantage of her, The only thing that would be left of the **DJ** would be that piece of Bambi's mom that he wears on his head!

To this day, I have not had the "Pleasure" of running into this "*Coward*" But I know, one day **He will have to answer for his actions!**

Because, after my experience with the wrong that I committed, I learned "Karma" is **real!**

And that, I got Mine, And, I believe BOTH of

them WILL GET THIERS TOO!

I would like (*as any of you would who had a person you were in a relationship with that went on to cheat on you with one of your "Friends"*)to see these 'Possible" scenarios for this *New couple*...

That the **DJ** would come home and find Tina *cheating on him* with a friend of his.
Or
Have the **DJ** come home and find Tina 'FUCKING" her dog.... (*Whom I suspected all along*)
Or even a better solution....

That they were both found in bed '***Deceased***" in the "**69**" position...And the cause of death was the 'toxic fumes' they secreted from each other!

Ahhhhh...what a 'Happy Ending" that would be...

But, as for this **DJ**, He turned out to be fake as the Hair-piece on his head! My label of '*Coward*" fits this 'prick! If he was a man, he would have told me about his interest in **The WHORE** back at the gas station when he told me to "Have a Nice

Holiday"…

The **DJ** knew about the problems that Tina and I were having. I remember the times I would talk to him about her cheating past, and about my fear that she was cheating in this relationship. I guess he used that information about our rocky relationship (*Tina and I*) to entice her to cheat on me!

With that, I will no longer (*as will others*) listen to the Radio Station that he works for. I learned (*from my own experiences*) No one should try and interfere in a relationship (*good or bad*) especially when that person comes into your life posing as a friend.

For all the good work that his station does for the community, it is a *SHAME* that they employ a person like that to represent their station! As for what station this DJ works for? Well, I could give you **105.1** guesses. And if you add a Little **MAGIC** you can figure it out yourself!

I will take a quote from one of the stations STAR Host. He stated; 'There is a Special place in **HELL** for Cheaters" And, after the HELL that I just endured, (*by cheating on my wife*) I would have to agree!

I have not talked to Tina since. But recently I walked into one of the local sports bars, and as I walked in…I noticed Tina sitting at a table to my right! I looked at her and noticed that she was not even close to the looks of the woman I met that fateful night in October…

Now she looked like, well …Like a **WHORE**! …Well, I did something that night, I should have done the first time I met this woman. I saw her, I said nothing to her, and I turned around, AND WALKED OUT of the Bar!

And back to my "friend" the **DJ**, I know that night at Denny's; I saved a *Good Woman (Miss Michigan)* from the **DJ'S** mysterious *Head of Hair* (**YUK!**). I guess she did not care what he had as far as Money or Fame…

Nor did she COMPROMISE HERSELF that night when she was vulnerable. She stayed faithful to her husband *(even though she had her suspicions of him being Unfaithful)*.

Yes, I feel Miss Michigan passed the Character test that evening.

To me, she was crowned THE WINNER!

And In the end, I was unwilling to stop the **DJ** from getting the WHORE.

Why you may ask?

Well, Based on THEIR CHARACTER, Those Two (**WHORES**) <u>ARE</u> MEANT TO BE TOGETHER!

Now …To complete the transfer of this *DISEASE*, I guess I have to give thanks … Just as Tina's Husband gave to me.

And, I guess it is "My Turn" to give the **DJ** a… **<u>HANDSHAKE!</u>**

<u>Closing</u>

Now, the Question to you is…
Are you willing to lose EVERYTHING for a
night with a "WHORE?"…

Because my friend, this could happen to you! Just
change the Name, and add your own name to this
main character!

Remember, I thought I had my life under control!
My friends, I would give ANYTHING not to have
been at that bar that fateful night….
But unfortunately, I was there!
  There are many WHORE'S lurking at your local
bars and clubs just looking to find someone that is
<u>'Vulnerable"</u> There are also websites advertising
places for married people to meet for a "discrete"
meeting for Sex!
  Just recently, A loving husband *(father of
three)* discovered on his wife's cell phone some
disturbing messages left by another man
(*I call that man…a Male WHORE.*)

I feel that with the *Promise of a better future* that our *New President* will bring to this Country we should ALL start looking at ourselves in the mirror about the choices we make in our relationships!

The Divorce rate in this country is at a **WHOPPING 50%** and climbing…

How can we expect other countries to respect us as a Nation under God, if we cannot follow the laws God has given to us in the *Commitment of Marriage*!

I might sound like a *hypocrite, but my friend, look where it landed me*….To this day, my Daughter does not want to see me. And, I am a lonely soul without her! I sleep through most of the HOLIDAYS because I do not have my Daughter there to share them with me….Because of *what I chose* to do!

Before I leave you, I want to show you how our 'morals" are compromised in this country….

Just for an example…

How successful is the marriage rate on the reality

show "The Bachelor" Are the women who appear for the six or so weeks really marriage material, or will they compromise themselves and really are WHORES?

Let me go a little further in what I mean about my above statement…

How about this Scenario…

For the next *Bachelor* who is in search for their true love…Let's (*for kicks*) *CHANGE* the setting to be as follows;

Instead of having these **25** single women fly out to *Las Vegas* to meet their *True Love*…
Let's instead, have them flown to the hometown of this man who is in search for the "Woman of his Dreams"…
Which in this scenario,
Will be his hometown of
Grand Rapids, MI…

And when they arrive, all **25** of the women will not *stay* in the **MGM GRAND HOTEL**,

But, at the local *Holiday Inn express…*
And, when they meet the possible true love of
their life, He greets them with a
"***Welcome to Bob Evans***" name tag on his work
shirt!

First of all, if the producers of the show were to
be 'Honest" about this possible scenario, they
would have a hard time finding women with a
Full set of Teeth to sign up for this show!

Secondly, if the producers were not Truthful to
the **25** women about the Arrangements to their
trip, I guarantee you THERE WILL BE A LOT
OF PISSED OFF WOMEN leaving on the first
Greyhound Bus BACK HOME!

*I believe…*If you are looking for real *True Love*
in your life, DO NOT use your WEALTH on your
resume to find them!   Yes, by all means tell them
that you are *employed*, but do not mention how
much you make, or how big your home is!

Please allow me to add one more example;

Do you think if *Hugh Hefner* did not have his
WEALTH that he would still be able to lure *Young*

Beautiful Supermodels into bed with him?
HELL No!

Picture this...
What If "Old Hef" was 'Down and Out" living off *welfare*? And, he lived in the *Detroit Projects*? Tell me, what *Beautiful Supermodels* would he attract then? *None*, that's right! He would be called an *Old Pervert* who just walks around the Neighborhood in his *Housecoat* and Pipe, Trying to Lure Young Ladies to sleep with him *for*....
Food Stamps!

<u>*Do you get the Message?*</u>

So, AS IN THE GLASS OF WINE...is your Relationship HALF FULL, or is it half EMPTY?

<u>*My Hope*</u> is with this Book, If
I can prevent just ONE Married Person from CHOOSING the **WHORE**. It would be as if
I Saved a Marriage
(*Even though I could not save my own*)...

If you do not heed my advice, Then you must not have any "Common Sense" and the label of an 'Idiot" is YOURS! So, remember this...

I Warned You!

Sorry but, there is no "Happy Ending" to MY story...

A Special thanks to: All of My "TRUE FRIENDS":
Sunny and William who helped guide me in the path to the Rebirth in Christ. Also, to Sean and his family., Peter, Mase, and their family, Cary, Tom Ging, Robert M, My Brothers Mark, George, My sister Kathy, and ...to My "Role Models"...My Aunt and Uncle, along with their family in Pittsburg... And, a special thanks to My "Good friend" Sandy!

I would like to thank Mariah Carey for the "Lifesaving" inspirational Song... (HERO)!

And finally, to my father James Longas (1926-1983), my mother Betty Longas (1926-1995), and my brother Gary Longas (1958-2003), YOU WILL ALWAYS BE MISSED!!!

Beware of the Whore

Beware of the Whore

Made in the USA
Middletown, DE
29 September 2023

39776106R00121